Personal Connections in the Digital Age

Digital Media and Society

Personal Connections in the Digital Age

NANCY K. BAYM

polity

First published in 2010 by Polity Press
Reprinted in 2011, 2012 (three times), 2013

Polity Press
65 Bridge Street
Cambridge CB2 1UR, UK

Polity Press
350 Main Street
Malden, MA 02148, USA

ISBN-13: 978-0-7456-4331-1
ISBN-13: 978-0-7456-4332-8 (pb)

A catalogue record for this book is available from the British Library.

Typeset in 9.5 on 12.5 pt FF Scala
by Servis Filmsetting Ltd, Stockport, Cheshire
Printed and bound in the USA by Edwards Brothers, Inc.

The publisher has used its best endeavours to ensure that the URLs for external websites referred to in this book are correct and active at the time of going to press. However, the publisher has no responsibility for the websites and can make no guarantee that a site will remain live or that the content is or will remain appropriate.

Every effort has been made to trace all copyright holders, but if any have been inadvertently overlooked the publisher will be pleased to include any necessary credits in any subsequent reprint or edition.

For further information on Polity, visit our website: www.politybooks.com

Contents

Illustrations

Acknowledgements

Thanks to my editor, Andrea Drugan, who approached me with the idea for one book and then responded with enthusiasm and encouragement when I suggested quite another. Thanks to those who read and provided feedback on drafts, including Nicole Ellison, Keith Hampton, and danah boyd. Holly Kruse, Adrianne Kunkel, Lynn Cherny, and Scott Campbell helped by pointing me to additional readings. Yan Bing Zhang, Mei-Chen Lin, Andrew Ledbetter, Kiley Larson, Adrianne Kunkel, Ryan Milner, and Michelle McCudden collaborated with me on some of my research discussed here. I also thank Kiley and Ryan for their editing and manuscript-preparation help. Markus Slivka has my eternal gratitude for letting me use him as an example and for his friendship. Joel Orff gets thanks both for drawing such a beautiful comic strip of our story and for granting me permission to reproduce it here. This book wouldn't be what it is without the students who have taken my undergraduate and graduate courses about personal relationships and new technology over the years at the University of Kansas. Finally, I wouldn't be who I am without my family, whose support sustains me face-to-face, online, over the phone, and on paper. I thank them most of all.

1

New forms of personal connection

There have never been more ways to communicate with one another than there are right now. Once limited to face to face conversation, over the last several millennia we have steadily developed new technologies for interaction. The digital age is distinguished by rapid transformations in the kinds of technological mediation through which we encounter one another. Face to face conversation, landline telephone calls, and postal mail have been joined by email, mobile phone calls, text messaging, instant messaging, chat, web boards, social networks, photo sharing, video sharing, multiplayer gaming, and more. People have always responded to new media with confusion. In this time of rapid innovation and diffusion, it's natural to be concerned about their effects on our relationships.

When first faced with a new barrage of interpersonal communication media, people tend to react in one of two ways, both of which have long cultural histories. On the one hand, people express concern that our communication has become increasingly shallow. For many, the increased amount of mediated interaction seems to threaten the sanctity of our personal relationships. For others, new media offer the promise of more opportunity for connection with more people, a route to new opportunities and to stronger relationships and more diverse connections. Both perspectives reflect a sense that digital media are changing the nature of our social connections. Over time, as people get used to new communication media, we come to see them in more nuanced ways. Eventually they become so taken for granted they are all but invisible. These moments in which they are new and the norms for their use are in flux offer fresh opportunities to think about our technologies, our connections, and the relationships amongst them.

The purpose of this book is to provide a means of thinking critically about the roles of digital media, in particular the internet and the mobile phone, in personal relationships. Rather than providing exuberant accounts or cautionary tales, this book provides a theoretical and data-grounded primer on how to make sense of these important changes in relational life. I began paying attention to these issues in 1990, launched my first research project into interpersonal communication over the internet in 1991, and began teaching courses in communication and new technology in Communication departments in 1994. The material in this book draws on my research projects, observations, and the large and growing body of scholarship on how digital media affect our interpersonal lives to offer frameworks for evaluating and understanding these changes.

New media, new boundaries

Digital media raise a variety of issues as we try to understand them, their place in our lives, and their consequences for our personhood and relationships with others. When they are new, technologies affect how we see the world, our communities, our relationships, and our selves. They lead to social and cultural reorganization and reflection. In her landmark study of nineteenth-century popular scientific magazines, Carolyn Marvin (1988) showed how a new technology such as electricity, the telegraph, or the telephone creates a point in history where the familiar becomes unfamiliar, and therefore open to change. This leads to anxiety. While people in ancient times fretted about writing and Victorians fretted about electricity, today we are in "a state of anxiety not only about the PC, but in relation to technology more generally" (D. Thomas, 2004: 219).

The fundamental purpose of communication technologies from their ancient inception has been to allow people to exchange messages without being physically co-present. Until the invention of the telegraph in the 1800s, this ability to transcend space brought with it inevitable time delays. Messages could take years to reach their audience. The telegraph changed that by allowing real-time communication across long distances for the first time. People may have reeled in the face of writing and publishing, but it was little compared to how we reeled and continued to reel in the face of this newfound power to collapse time and space. After millennia as creatures who engage in social interaction face to face, the ability to communicate across distance at very high speeds disrupts social understandings that are burned deep into our collective conscience. Digital media continue these disruptions and pose new ones. They raise important questions for scholars and lay people alike. How can we be present yet also absent? What is a self if it's not in a body? How can we have so much control yet lose so much freedom? What does personal communication mean when it's transmitted through a mass medium? What's a mass medium if it's used for personal communication? What do private and public mean anymore? What does it even mean to *be* real?

Kenneth Gergen (2002) describes us as struggling with the "challenge of absent presence," worrying that too often we inhabit a "floating world" in which we engage primarily with non-present partners despite the presence of flesh-and-blood people in our physical location. We may be physically present in one space, yet mentally and emotionally engaged elsewhere. Consider, for instance, the dinner partner who is immersed in his mobile phone conversation. Since he is physically present, yet simultaneously absent, the very nature of self becomes problematic. Where is "he?" The borders between human and machine, the collapse of which was celebrated in Haraway's (1990) "Cyborg manifesto," and between self and body, are thrown into flux. In a time when some people feel that their "real self" is expressed best online (McKenna, Green, & Gleason, 2002), long-distance romances are built and maintained through electronic contact, and spaces for our media are built right into the clothing we wear, how do we know where, exactly, true selves reside? Furthermore, what if the selves enacted through digital media don't line up with those we present face to face, or if they contradict one another? If someone is nurturing face to face, aggressive in one online forum, and needy in another online forum, which is real? Is there such a thing as a true self anymore? Was there ever?

The separation of presence from communication offers us more control over our social worlds yet simultaneously subjects us to new forms of control, surveillance, and constraint. Naomi Baron (2008) argues that new media offer us "volume control" to regulate our social environment and manage our encounters. We can create new opportunities to converse. We can avoid interactions, talking into a mobile phone (or pretending to) to avoid a co-present acquaintance or letting calls go to voice mail. We can manipulate our interactions, doing things like forwarding nasty emails or putting people on speakerphone. We can use nonverbally limited media such as text messages or emails to shelter us from anxiety-inducing encounters such as flirting or ending relationships. But, just as we can use these media to manage others more strategically, others can also more easily manage us. Our autonomy is increasingly constrained by the expectation that we can be reached for communication anytime, anywhere, and we will owe an appropriate and timely response. We are trapped by the same state of "perpetual contact" (Katz & Aakhus, 2002) that empowers us.

One of the most exciting elements of new media is that they allow us to communicate personally within what used to be prohibitively large groups. This blurs the boundary between mass and interpersonal communication in ways that disrupt both. When people gather in an online space to talk about a television show, they are a mass communication audience, but the communication they have with one another is both interpersonal, directed to individuals within the group, and mass, available for anyone to read. If, as increasingly happens, the conversations and materials these fans produce for one another are incorporated into the television show, the boundaries between the production and reception of mass media are blurred as well. Furthermore, what is personal may become mass, as when a young woman creates a videolog for her friends, which becomes widely viewed on YouTube. The ability for individuals to communicate and produce mediated content on a mass scale has led to opportunities for fame that were not available outside of the established culture industries before, but confusion about the availability and scale of messages has also led to unplanned broadcast of what was meant to be private.

This is just one way in which the boundaries between public and private are implicated in and changed by digital media. Internet users, especially youth, have been decried for revealing private information through online activities. Mobile phone users have been assailed for carrying on private conversations in public spaces (and shooting nasty looks at those who don't pretend not to notice). Puro (2002: 23) describes mobile phone users as "doubly privatizing" public space since they "sequester themselves non-verbally and then fill the air with private matters." Homes, especially in affluent societies, exhibit a "privatized media rich bedroom culture" (Livingstone, 2005) in which people use media to create privacy and solitude. All of this happens in a cultural moment when individualism is increasingly defined through consumerist practices of purchasing mass mediated and branded products (Gergen, 1991; Livingstone, 2005; Walker, 2008).

At the heart of this boundary flux is deep confusion about what is virtual – that which seems real but is ultimately a mere simulation – and what is real. Even people who hang out and build relationships online contrast it to what they do "IRL" (In Real Life), lending credence to the perception that the mediated is unreal. Digital media thus call into question the very authenticity of our identities, relationships, and practices (e.g. Sturken & Thomas, 2004). Some critics have noted that these disruptions are part and parcel of a movement from modern to postmodern times in which time and space are compressed, speed is accelerated, people are ever more mobile, communication is person-to-person rather than place-to-place, identities are multiple, and communication media are ubiquitous (e.g. Fornås, Klein, Ladendorf, Sundén, & Sveningsson, 2002; Haythornthwaite & Wellman, 2002; Ling, 2004). Others have emphasized how, within these cultural changes, digital media are made mundane, boring, and routine as they are increasingly embedded in everyday lives and social norms coalesce around their use (e.g. Haythornthwaite & Wellman, 2002; Humphreys, 2005; Ling, 2004). The first perspective forms a necessary backdrop for contextualizing and making sense of the second, but the emphasis in this book is on the mundane and the everyday, on how people incorporate digital media into their routine practices of relating and with what consequences.

Plan of the book

In the remainder of this chapter I identify a set of key concepts that can be used to differentiate digital media and which influence how people use them and with what effects. I then offer a very brief overview of the media discussed in this book and a discussion of who does and who doesn't make use of them. Chapter 2 is an orientation to the major perspectives used to understand the interrelationships between communication technology and society and an exploration of the major themes in popular rhetorics about digital media and personal connection. Chapter 3 examines what happens to messages, both verbal and nonverbal, in mediated contexts. Chapter 4 addresses the group contexts in which online interaction often happens, including communities and social networks. The remaining two chapters explore dyadic relationships. Chapter 5 shows how people present themselves to others and first get to know each other online. Chapter 6 looks at how people use new media to build and maintain their relationships. Finally, the conclusion returns to the question of sorting myths from reality, arguing against the notion of a "cyberspace" that can be understood apart from the mundane realities of everyday life and for the notion that what happens online may be newer, but is no less real.

Seven key concepts

If we want to build a rich understanding of how media influence personal connections, we need to stop talking about media in overly simplistic terms. We can't talk about consequences if we can't articulate capabilities. What is it about these media that changes interaction and, potentially, relationships? We need conceptual tools to differentiate media from one another and from face to face (or, as Fortunati, 2005, more aptly termed it, "body to body") communication. We also need concepts to help us recognize the diversity amongst what may seem to be just one technology. The mobile phone, for instance, is used for voice, texting, and also picture and video exchange. The internet includes interaction platforms as diverse as YouTube, product reviews on shopping sites, email and Instant Messaging (IM), which differ from one another in many ways. Seven concepts that can be used to productively compare different media to one another as well as to face to face communication are interactivity, temporal structure, social cues, storage, replicability, reach, and mobility.

The many modes of communication on the internet and mobile phone vary in the degrees and kinds of *interactivity* they offer. Consider, for instance, the difference between using your phone to select a new ringtone and using that phone to argue with a romantic partner, or using a web site to buy new shoes rather than to discuss current events. Fornäs and his co-authors (2002: 23) distinguish several meanings of interactivity. Social interactivity, "the ability of a medium to enable social interaction between groups or individuals," is what we are most interested in here. Other kinds include technical interactivity, "a medium's capability of letting human users manipulate the machine via its interface," and textual interactivity, "the creative and interpretive interaction between users (readers, viewers, listeners) and texts." "Unlike television," writes Laura Gurak (2001: 44), "online communication technologies allow you to talk back. You can talk back to the big company or you can talk back to individual citizens." Rafaeli and Sudweeks (1997) posit that we should see interactivity as a continuum enacted by people using technology, rather than a technological condition. As we will see in chapters to come, the fact that the internet enables interactivity gives rise to new possibilities – for instance, we can meet new people and remain close to those who have moved away – as well as old concerns that people may be flirting with danger.

The *temporal structure* of a communication medium is also important. Synchronous communication, such as is found in face to face conversations, phone calls, and instant messages, occurs in real time. Asynchronous communication media, such as email and voicemail, have time delays between messages. In practice, the distinction cannot always be tied to specific media. Poor connections may lead to time delays in a seemingly synchronous online medium such as Instant Messaging. Text messaging via the telephone is often asynchronous, but needn't be. Ostensibly asynchronous email may be sent and received so rapidly that it functions as a synchronous mode of communication.

The beauty of synchronous media is that they allow for the very rapid transmission of messages, even across distance. As we will see, synchronicity can enhance the sense of placelessness that digital media can encourage and make people feel more together when they are apart (Baron, 1998; Carnevale & Probst, 1997; McKenna & Bargh, 1998). Synchronicity can make messages feel more immediate and personal (O'Sullivan, Hunt, & Lippert, 2004) and encourage playfulness in interaction (Danet, 2001). The price of synchronicity, however, is that interactants must be able to align their schedules in order to be simultaneously engaged. Real-time media are also poorly suited to hosting interaction in large groups, as the rapid-fire succession of messages that comes from having many people involved is nearly impossible to sort through and comprehend, let alone answer. There is a reason that dinner parties are generally kept to a small collection of people and at large functions guests are usually seated at tables that seat fewer than a dozen. Accordingly, most online chat rooms and other real-time forums have limits on how many can participate at one time.

With asynchronous media, the costs and benefits are reversed. Asynchronous communication allows very large groups to sustain interaction, as seen in the social network sites and online groups like fan forums, support groups, and hobbyist communities addressed in chapter 4. Asynchronicity also gives people time to manage their self-presentations more strategically. However, word may filter more slowly through such groups and amongst individuals. We can place fewer demands on others' time by leaving asynchronous messages for people to reply to when they like, but we may end up waiting longer than we'd hoped, or receive no reply at all. One of the biggest changes wrought by digital media is that even asynchronous communication can happen faster than before. Time lags are created by the time it takes a person to check for new messages and respond, not by the time messages spend in transit. In comparison to postal mail, the internet can shave weeks off interactions.

Most of the questions surrounding the personal connections

people form and maintain through digital media derive from the sparse *social cues* that are available to provide further information regarding context, the meanings of messages, and the identities of the people interacting. As chapter 3 will address in more detail, rich media provide a full range of cues, while leaner media provide fewer. Body-to-body, people have a full range of communicative resources available to them. They share a physical context, which they can refer to nonverbally as well as verbally (for instance, by pointing to a chair). They are subject to the same environmental influences and distractions. They can see one another's body movements, including the facial expressions through which so much meaning is conveyed. They can use each other's eye gaze to gauge attention. They can see one another's appearance. They can also hear the sound of one another's voice. All of these cues – contextual, visual, and auditory – are important to interpreting messages and creating a social context within which messages are meaningful.

To varying degrees, digital media provide fewer social cues. In mobile and online interactions, we may have few if any cues to our partner's location. This is no doubt why so many mobile phone calls begin with the question "where are you?" and also helps to explain some people's desire to share GPS positioning via mobile applications. The lack of shared physical context does not mean that interactants have no shared contexts. People communicating in personal relationships share relational contexts, knowledge, and some history. People in online groups often develop rich in-group social environments that those who've participated for any length of time will recognize.

Though, as we will address in more depth in chapter 6, much of our mediated interaction is with people we know face to face, some media convey very little information about the identities of those with whom we are communicating. In some circumstances, this renders people anonymous, leading to both opportunity and terror. In lean media, people have more ability to expand, manipulate, multiply, and distort the identities they present to others. The paucity of personal and social identity cues can also make people feel safer, and thus create an environment in which they are more honest. Chapter 5 examines these identity issues.

Media also differ in the extent to which their messages endure. *Storage*, and, relatedly, *replicability*, are highly consequential. Unless one makes an audio or video recording of telephone and face to face conversations (practices with laws governing acceptable practice), they are gone as soon as they are said. Human memory for conversation is notoriously poor. To varying degrees, digital media may be stored on devices, web sites, and company backups where they may be replicated, retrieved at later dates, and edited prior to sending (Carnevale & Probst, 1997; Cherny, 1999; Culnan & Markus, 1987; Walther, 1996). Synchronous forms like IM and Skype require logging programs that most users are not likely to have. Those that are asynchronous can be easily saved, replicated and redistributed to others. They can also be archived for search. Despite this, online messages may feel ephemeral, and indeed web sites may be there one day and different or gone the next.

Media also vary in the size of an audience they can attain or support, or *reach*. Gurak (2001: 30) describes reach as "the partner of speed," noting that "digitized discourse travels quickly, but it also travels widely . . . One single keystroke can send a message to thousands of people." Face to face communication is inherently limited to those who can fit in the same space. Even when amplified (a form of mediation in itself), physical space and human sensory constraints limit how many can see or hear a message as it's delivered. The telephone allows for group calls, but the upper limit on how many a group can admit or maintain is small. In contrast, many forms of digital communication can be seen by any internet user (as in the case of websites) or can be sent and, thanks to storage and replicability, resent to enormous audiences. Messages can reach audiences both local and global. This is a powerful subversion of the elitism of mass media, within which a very small number of broadcasters could engage in one-to-many communication, usually within regional or geographic boundaries. The gatekeeping function of mass media is challenged as individuals use digital media to spread messages much farther and more widely than was ever historically possible (Gurak, 2001). Future chapters will address how enhanced reach allows people to form new communities of interest and new relationships.

Finally, media vary in their *mobility*, or extent to which they are portable – enabling people to send and receive messages regardless of location – or stationary – requiring that people be in specific locations in order to interact. The mobile phone represents the paradigm case of mobility, making person-to-person communication possible regardless of location. The clunky personal computer tied to a desk requires that the user be seated in that spot. Landline phones require that people be in the building where that number rings. In addition to offering spatial mobility, some digital media allow us to move between times and interpersonal contexts (Ishii, 2006). Mobile media offer the promise that we need never be out of touch with our loved ones, no matter how long the traffic jam in which we find ourselves. When stuck with our families, we may import our friends through our mobile devices. As we'll see in chapter 6, mobile media give rise to microcoordination (Ling, 2004) in which people check in with one another to provide brief updates or quickly arrange meetings and errands. However, more than other personal media, mobile phones threaten autonomy, as we may become accountable to others at all times. Schegloff (2002), one of the first to study telephone-mediated interaction, suggests mobile media don't create perpetual contact so much as offer the perpetual possibility of making contact, a distinction some exploit by strategically limiting their availability (Licoppe & Heurtin, 2002).

These seven concepts help us begin to understand the similarities and differences between face to face communication and mediated interaction, as well as the variation amongst different kinds of digital interactions. Face to face communication, like all the forms of digital media we will be discussing, is interactive. People can respond to one another in message exchanges. Face to face communication is synchronous. It is also loaded with social cues that make one another's identities and many elements of social and physical context apparent (although, as we will return to in chapter 5, this does not guarantee honesty). Face to face conversations cannot be stored, nor can they be replicated. Even when recorded and, for example, broadcast, the recording loses many elements of the context that make face to face communication what it is. As discussed above, face to face communication has low reach, limiting how many can be involved and how far messages can spread. Face to face communication may be mobile, but only so long as the interactants are moving through space together. This combination of qualities grants face to face a sort of specialness. The full range of cues, the irreplicability, and the need to be there in shared place and time with the other all contribute to the sense that face to face communication is authentic, putting the "communion" in communication.

In contrast, some forms of mediated interaction are asynchronous, enabling more message planning and wider reach, but a potentially lower sense of connection. Media such as Skype or other video chat technologies offer many social cues – voice, facial expression, a window into the physical surroundings – but lack critical intimacy cues including touch and smell. Most digital media have fewer social cues than that, limiting interaction to sounds or even just words. By virtue of their conversion into electronic signals, all digital media can be stored, though particular interactions may not be. Even when conversations and messages are not stored, however, they may leave traces such as records of which phone numbers called which other ones, which IP addresses visited which websites, or how many tweets a person has twittered. Digital messages are easily replicated if they are asynchronous, but less so if they are synchronous. The reach of digital media can vary tremendously depending on the medium. A phone call generally remains a one-to-one encounter as does much instant messaging and chat, but emails, mailing lists, discussion groups, and websites are among the digital modes that can have extraordinary reach. Digital media are becoming increasingly mobile as the internet and mobile phone converge into single devices, meaning that these technologies make communication possible in places where it wasn't before, but also that they can intrude into face to face conversations where they never could before. As a result, people can have very different experiences with different media, yet none may seem to offer the potential for intimacy and connection that being face to face does. These distinctions all bring with them important potential social shifts, which the remainder of this book will address.

Digital media

Just as it's important to clarify core concepts that may shape medi-ated social interaction, it's helpful to walk through the media in question. I assume readers are familiar with the mobile phone, so I focus below on a brief historical overview of the internet. I empha-size the extent to which the interpersonal appeal of these media shaped their development. Unlike the mobile phone, the internet was not built as a personal communication medium, let alone a way for fans to connect around their objects of pleasure, for people to find potential romantic partners, for employers to find or investi-gate potential hires, or any such social processes. It was developed to safeguard military knowledge. When the first internet connec-tion was made in 1969 through what was then called ARPANET, funded by the US Department of Defense, no one envisioned that an interpersonal communication medium had been launched. It is beyond the scope of this book to cover the technological develop-ment of the internet; the reader is referred to Janet Abbate's (1999) history. First, though, a disclaimer: trying to list specific types of digital media is frustrating at best. Between this writing and your reading there are bound to be new developments, and things popular as I write will drop from vogue. Let this be a reminder to us of the importance of remaining focused on specific capabilities and consequences rather than the media themselves.

The textual internet

For its first quarter-century, the internet was text-only. With its limited social cues, it seemed a poor match for personal interac-tion. Yet it took mere months for its developers (who were also its primary users) to realize the medium's utility for personal com-munication. Within three years of the first login, email was in use, and within four years, three-quarters of online traffic was email (Anderson, 2005). By 2000, the ability to use email was a signifi-cant reason that people first got online and one of the main reasons that those already online stayed online (Kraut, Mukhopadhyay, Szczypula, Kiesler, & Scherlis, 2000).

Synchronous person-to-person and small-group communication also developed early in the internet's history. "Talk" was an early synchronous internet communication genre. When using Talk, a horizontal line divided the top and lower halves of the screen, each half showing messages from one interactant. It was as minimalist and purely textual as a communication medium could be. Talk remained in regular usage into the early 1990s. When I began using the internet in 1990, I used it almost daily to tell my then-boyfriend that dinner was ready – I couldn't call since his phone line was tied up with his modem's internet connection. Talk provided a convenient work-around. Talk was followed by Internet Relay Chat (IRC) and, later, chat rooms that allowed distributed groups to converse in real-time. Instant Messaging, developed in the 1990s, can be seen as an advanced version of Talk. A person-to-person medium, IM is distinctive in its use of a buddy list and provision of continual information about who on that list is online and available for contact.

Not long after email, mailing lists were developed, in which a single email could be sent to a large group of subscribers, all of whom would receive it and (usually) be able to respond. Although the technological specifications of email and mailing lists are the same, there are some important differences. Specifically, on mailing lists, senders may very well not know most (or any) of the recipients. Mailing lists are often large. For instance, the Association of Internet Researchers' mailing list, AIR-L, has approximately 2,000 subscribers in many nations. In contrast, others are small private lists of family and friends. A colleague of mine, faced with a family member's cancer, created a mailing list of family members so that they could all share news with a single message. Private mailing lists may also be made up of school friends who have graduated or other such small groups of people seeking to stay in touch as a group.

In the early 1980s, another means of asynchronous group discussion with wide reach developed. Usenet newsgroups are asynchronous topic-based discussion forums distributed across multiple servers. Although these groups have become magnets for spam, they continue to house a great deal of online discussion. Originally, one read newsgroups through newsreaders built into

Unix operating systems. This later developed into stand-alone newsreaders. Now most people access Usenet through the web, most notably through Google groups, where they may well not recognize them as Usenet newsgroups. These provided an early model for the topical web boards so common now. They were also my own entrée into online group communication and the subject of my earliest work on computer mediated communication.

In some early sites, developers and participants used words and code to create a rich geographical context for synchronous interactions and a highly developed range of characters. In the late 1970s, Richard Bartle and Roy Trubshaw developed MUD1, an interactive online role-playing game. Around the same time, Alan Klietz independently developed Sceptre of Goth, a MUD game (Bartle, 2004). Readers who play World of Warcraft or related massively multiplayer online role-playing games will recognize MUDs as their precedent. MUD stands for either Multi-User Domain or the less antiseptic Multi-User Dungeon, which better captures the phenomenon's origin in the role-playing game Dungeons and Dragons. Many MUDs offered predetermined categories by which to define one's character. People might choose their sex (often from a list with more than two choices) and race. Depending on the MUD, people might choose to be elves, fairies, cats, dragons, trolls, vampires, and other fantasy creatures.

Lambda MOO (Multi-User Domain Object-Oriented, a distinction that is of minimal importance here) and many other MUDs, MOOs, MUCKs, MUSHes, and other oddly acronymed parallel sites followed, many of which were simply creative environments in which fictional rooms and landscapes served as spaces for social interaction, not games. Though MUDs and MOOs have always been obscure uses of the internet (unlike the later graphical games they inspired), they were the object of an inordinate amount of early research about the internet.

The World Wide Web

A major transformation in digital communication occurred in the 1990s when a group of physicists led by Sir Tim Berners-Lee at the

Swiss physics laboratory CERN developed the World Wide Web. This heralded a shift from communication that was purely text-based to multimedia communication, and gave rise to more new forms of mediated interaction than I can cover here. These include web boards, blogs, wikis, social network sites, video and photo sharing sites, and graphically intensive virtual worlds.

In the 1990s, web boards took up where the promise of Usenet left off, facilitating asynchronous topic-based group interaction amongst people who did not need prior connections. Blogs, authored by either single people or collectives, are websites in which recent updates appear above previous updates, creating a reverse chronology of messages. Their content may be personal, political, or anything else, and their audiences may be anything from zero to millions. By convention and design, blogs almost always include a list of hyperlinks to other blogs (a "blog roll"), which serves to create connections and drive traffic amongst blogs. Groups of bloggers may read one another and comment on each others' blogs, creating communities of like-minded individuals and semi-organized grassroots social movements.

Also during this time, websites such as Active Worlds began to develop graphically rich environments. These have exploded in the early 2000s, in the form of massively multiplayer online role-playing games (MMORPGs – an acronym usually pronounced "more pigs") such as World of Warcraft, Everquest, and Lineage, and non-game spaces such as Second Life.

The 2000s brought with them what has been called "Web 2.0." The hallmark of Web 2.0 is often taken to be user-generated content, but, having been through the paragraphs just above, one must wonder what content on the textual internet and much of Web 1.0 was not generated by users. Wikis, the most famous of which is Wikipedia, are among the stars of this generation of digital media. Wikis are collective encyclopedia-authoring sites in which people can collaborate to produce informative entries. Though this may sound sterile, behind the editing of entries are rich social worlds of interconnected users with shared histories, conventions, and practices. Social network sites (SNSs) such as Facebook, MySpace, LiveJournal and Bebo, in which individuals have profiles to which they can upload many diverse media (photos, videos, music, links, and more) and connect their profiles with others through "friending", have been wildly successful in the 2000s and are near-ubiquitous, especially amongst young people, in some countries. boyd and Ellison (2007) locate the origins of SNSs in the advent of SixDegrees.com in 1997, followed by AsianAvenue, BlackPlanet and MiGente, then LiveJournal and Cyworld (1999) and LunarStorm (2000). MySpace began in 2003, and Facebook in 2005. Video and photo sharing sites such as YouTube (owned by Google) and Flickr (owned by Yahoo!) may be considered a subset of SNSs. In these sites, people can create personal accounts, upload their own materials, and share them with others publicly or only amongst approved recipients. Social network sites are unique in combining multiple modes of communication and, hence, in the breadth of and control over social cues they may provide.

As this brief review suggests, even as we are concerned with their overall impact, we must avoid the temptation to look at new media only as a whole. Each of these media, as well as the mobile phone, offers unique affordances, or packages of potentials and constraints, for communication. To understand how we use them, and with what consequences, we need to consider them both separately and holistically.

Who uses new digital media?

The story of online media history is also a story of changing users, and we need to keep questions of whom we are talking about in mind as we think about how new media and social life intertwine. In its early years, the only people using the internet were the ones developing it, almost all of whom were located in the United States and the UK (Abbate, 1999). By the 1980s, scientists at universities had begun to use it, and, by the end of that decade, college students were using it too. But the internet of the 1980s was funded almost entirely by the National Science Foundation (NSF), an agency of the United States government. Commercial activity was prohibited, and almost all users gained access through a university affiliation, or a government lab or agency. Computer networks connecting people with home computers, such as Compuserve, Prodigy, and America Online, began in the 1980s, as did many private electronic bulletin boards (indeed, these had existed since the 1970s). These provided home hobbyists with a means to get online, but they were not integrated with each other or with the internet.

Throughout the 1980s and the early 1990s, access to the internet gradually spread to other countries. It was not until the mid-1990s that the diffusion of the internet into everyday life for many Americans and people in some other parts of the world (most notably the UK and northern Europe) began in earnest. The years 1994 and 1995 were huge for the internet. The NSF pulled out of its funding, making commercial activity feasible, and the World Wide Web moved from concept to realization. Internet Service Providers such as America Online began to connect to the internet, and Americans began to come online in droves, leading to all kinds of culture clashes between those who had been online for years and this new class of users. By the end of the decade, most Americans were online.

Globally, the story is different, however, as it remains within some segments of the American population. Online media are far from universal, either across or within populations. Many books and articles have been written addressing the issues of the "digital divide" (e.g. Norris, 2001; Warschauer, 2004). As a whole, digital divide research has little to say about interpersonal connection, the topic of this book. Its focus is usually on issues such as political participation, career advancement, and the use of financial and health information (e.g. Hargittai & Hinnant, 2008). This research indicates that those most able to use new media are able to use them to improve their lives in ways that those who do not use them are not, increasing social and economic disparity. Everything this book will discuss needs to be understood as happening in a context which only some sectors of the global population can access or engage.

The digital divide is often framed as a simple division between those who have access to the internet and those who do not. Even within countries, there are clear trends in which populations use the internet and which don't. Within United States, survey research by the Pew Internet & American Life Project (*Who's Online*, 2009) has consistently found demographic differences in which adult Americans use the internet. In their April, 2009, random phone survey of American adults, more men than women used the internet (81 percent vs. 77 percent), and Whites were 12 percent more likely to use it than Blacks, though 5 percent less likely than English-speaking Hispanics. Among young people (18–29 years old) 92 percent used the internet, while only 42 percent of those over 65 did. Income also correlated strongly with internet use. Only 60 percent of people in households earning less than $30,000/year reported using the internet, while 95 percent of those earning $75,000 or more did. Education was also an influence, as those who had not graduated from high school reported 50 percent usage compared to the 94 percent of those who had graduated from college. Finally, location matters. People living in urban and suburban communities were 10–12 percent more likely to use the internet than people living in rural areas.

Globally, the disparities are even more striking. The website Internet World Stats (Miniwatts Marketing Group, 2009), which tracks this, estimates that 73.9 percent of North Americans use the internet, 60.1 percent of those in Oceania/Australia do, 50.1 percent of Europeans, 30 percent in Latin American / Caribbean countries, 23.7 percent of Middle Easterners, 18.5 percent of Asians, and only 6.7 percent of Africans. On average, just under a quarter of the world's population use the internet. Within these parts of the world, the factors that affect Americans (education, gender, age, etc.) affect further which members of the population are among the internet users.

In many regions where internet use is lower than in North America, mobile phone use is far more pervasive. A study released by the United Nations' International Telecommunications Union (2009) estimated that, while only 23 percent of the world's population used the internet, 61.1 percent used mobile phones, driven especially by use in Brazil, Russia, India, and China. The report also draws attention to the fact that not all internet is the same – only 6.1 percent of the global population have access to broadband services through a fixed internet connection, and only 5 percent have it through mobile connections. In the developing world, less than 2.4 percent of the population have any broadband access to the internet. The Pew Internet and American Life Project (Horrigan & Rainie, 2002) found that broadband access is important in shaping whether a person merely reads the internet or contributes content to it.

A 2001 UN Human Development Report is no doubt outdated in its precise numbers, but their analysis of global trends is still apt (UN, 2001). Much of the global population is illiterate, excluding them from much online participation. Worldwide, most internet users remain male, college-educated, and earn higher-than-average incomes. Women are in the minority of users in both developed and developing countries. For example, their report found that only 38 percent of internet users in Latin America were women, while in the European Union the figure was 25 percent, in Russia 19 percent, in Japan 18 percent, and in the Middle East 4 percent.

As the point about broadband suggests, access does not tell the whole story. Even if one sometimes uses a medium, other factors affect how much one is likely to gain from its use. Jung, Qiu, and Kim (2001) developed the Internet Connectedness Index to assess the varying degrees of connectivity that "internet use" may actually entail. Among the variables they identified as important were whether or not one owned a home computer, for how long one had owned one, from how many places a person could access the internet, how much time people spend online, and how many things a person can do online. Howard, Rainie, and Jones (2001) distinguish "netizens" from other users. They defined netizens as people who had been online for at least three years and who go online from home every day. Netizens, they found, are most likely to obtain resources that can improve their lives through the internet.

Eszter Hargittai's work has pointed to the importance of skill. Hargittai (2002) describes a "second level digital divide" that speaks to the differences in skill levels (e.g. understanding internet terminology, searching for and evaluating information) that internet users may have. Hargittai and Hinnant (2008) surveyed a random sample of US young adults. They found that women, people who had not graduated from college, and those who did not use the internet at home reported lower skill levels and were less likely to visit sites with the potential to improve one's life, such as those offering news, or government, health, financial, and product information sites.

In sum, we are still standing on shifting ground in our efforts to make sense of the capabilities of digital media and their social consequences. New media are constantly developing, new populations are taking up these tools, and new uses are emerging. Who is excluded from or enabled by digitally mediated interaction is neither random nor inconsequential. The same tools may take on very different meanings for different populations in different contexts or different times. It is too soon to tell what the final consequences will be, but it seems unlikely that they will ever be universal or stable. In the rest of this book we'll work with what data we have to fill in what we know now. I hope that astute readers will read between the lines to consider also how much more we have to learn.

2

Making new media make sense

When faced with a new communication medium, the immediate challenge for scholars, users, and non-users is to make sense of it. What is it good for? What are its risks? What benefits might it bring? To understand new media, we need to consider both the technological features of a medium and the personal, cultural, and historical presumptions and values those features evoke. In the last chapter, I raised the notion that new media cause cultural anxieties and articulated several technological concepts that help us to think about how new media may differ from earlier forms of communication as well as from one another. Most anxieties around both digital media and their historical precursors stem from the fact that these media are interactive. Especially in combination with sparse social cues, interactivity raises issues about the authenticity and well-being of people, interactions, and relationships that use new media. Other anxieties arise out of the temporal structure of digital media, which seem to push us towards continuous interaction. The internet's ability to store and replicate information without regard to its content leads to fears about what that content might include and how this power might be abused in harmful ways. The mobility of some new media means that we can now have conversations that would have once been held in our homes when we are in public and that we can be with others wherever we are, feeding into a related set of concerns about privacy and companionship.

In addition to technological qualities, social qualities also shape the anxieties we have and the questions we pose about new communication technologies. This chapter explores the messages that circulate around new media in order to show how social forces influence technological interpretation and use. New media appear in the stories we tell each other about what happened during our day and in the domestic squabbles over whose turn it is to use the computer. They are also represented in mass media, where technologies play starring and peripheral roles in news stories, magazine articles, films, and television shows. Popular films such as *You've Got Mail* or *The Net*, both released shortly after the internet became popular in the USA, provide modern-day fairy tales that serve as cultural referents for understanding online romance or identity theft. The messages in popular media, examples of which we'll see below, show the social elements we bring to understanding new communication technologies and help to shape how people understand new technology.

Through communication, people assign symbolic meanings to technologies. The messages we communicate about technology are *reflective*, revealing as much about the communicators as they do about the technology (Sturken & Thomas, 2004). When we communicate about digital media, we are communicating about ourselves, as individuals, groups, and societies. As we represent these unfamiliar interpersonal tools through our words, conversations, stories, metaphors, images, and so on, we collectively negotiate what interpersonal relationships are and what we want them to be. When we talk about technology, we are sharing "the visions, both optimistic and anxious, through which modern societies cohere" (Sturken & Thomas, 2004: 1). In addition to telling us about a medium, communication about technology is also one of the best places to see "the desires and concerns of a given social context and the preoccupations of particular moments in history" (Sturken & Thomas, 2004: 1).

Communication about technology is also *productive*, generating new meanings for technologies, new uses of technologies, and even new technologies (Sturken & Thomas, 2004). As early as the sixteenth century, there was an urban legend about "sympathetic needles" that allowed people to communicate instantaneously across distance, a legend that helped to inspired the telegraph (Standage, 1998). In our own time, William Gibson's 1984 science fiction novel *Neuromancer* gave us the term "cyberspace," and both his writings and those of Neal Stephenson, especially the novel

Snow Crash (1992), provided models of virtual worlds such as Second Life that were developed in their aftermath.

When people explain the consequences of a new medium in terms of technological, social, or some combination of these forces, they rely on theoretical assumptions about causality. This chapter is organized around the major theoretical frameworks for understanding the causal flow between technology and society. There is a strong tendency, especially when technologies are new, to view them as causal agents, entering societies as active forces of change that humans have little power to resist. This perspective is known as *technological determinism*. When media are new, most popular messages about them are deterministic. A second perspective, the *social construction of technology*, argues that people are the primary sources of change in both technology and society. The *social shaping* perspective sees influence as flowing in both directions. Ultimately, over time, people stop questioning individual technologies. Through a process of *domestication*, they become taken-for-granted parts of everyday life, no longer seen as agents of change. In the remainder of this chapter, we'll look at each of these four perspectives, drawing on rhetorics of technologies old and new to illustrate how they work.

Technological determinism

Machines change us

In a widely read essay in the *Atlantic* (2008), Nick Carr posited that Google is "making us stupid." Before discussing other people's stories and neuroscience, he described his own dumbing down:

> Over the past few years I've had an uncomfortable sense that someone, or something, has been tinkering with my brain, remapping the neural circuitry, reprogramming the memory. My mind isn't going – so far as I can tell – but it's changing. I'm not thinking the way I used to think. I can feel it most strongly when I'm reading. Immersing myself in a book or a lengthy article used to be easy. My mind would get caught up in the narrative or the turns of the argument, and I'd spend hours strolling through long stretches of prose. That's rarely the case anymore. Now my concentration often starts

to drift after two or three pages. I get fidgety, lose the thread, begin looking
for something else to do.

As Carr tells it, "someone, or something," changed him. He
was the passive recipient transformed by an outside force. As he
himself articulates, Carr's essay is in keeping with a long-standing
tradition of technological determinism in which the technology is
conceptualized as an external agent that acts upon and changes
society.

A year after Carr worried that Google was sapping our intelligence, widespread news coverage of a forthcoming academic
lecture compared Facebook's ability to "enhance intelligence"
with Twitter's power to "diminish it." The UK paper the *Telegraph*
(Cockroft, 2009) described University of Stirling memory expert
Tracy Alloway's take on how asynchronous and synchronous
interaction online differentially affect the brain:

> Sudoku also stretched the working memory, as did keeping up with friends
> on Facebook, she said. But the "instant" nature of texting, Twitter and
> YouTube was not healthy for working memory. "On Twitter you receive
> an endless stream of information, but it's also very succinct," said Dr
> Alloway. "You don't have to process that information. Your attention span
> is being reduced and you're not engaging your brain and improving nerve
> connections."

Problematic as they may be, concerns like this should not be
dismissed. However, they should be understood in the theoretical
and historical context of the reception of new technologies. Popular
visions of new technology have tended towards technological
determinism as far back as Ancient Greece. Socrates (as quoted
by Plato, *c.*370 BCE) decried the invention of the alphabet and
writing as a threat to the oral tradition of Greek society (Ong,
1982). Anticipating what his nation's newspapers would write
1,000 years later (Koutsogiannis & Mitsikopoulou, 2003, to whom
we will return in the next chapter), Socrates warned the inventors
of the alphabet:

> this discovery of yours will create forgetfulness in the learners' souls,
> because they will not use their memories; they will trust to the external
> written characters and not remember of themselves. The specific which

you have discovered is an aid not to memory, but to reminiscence, and you give your disciples not truth, but only the semblance of truth; they will be hearers of many things and will have learned nothing; they will appear to be omniscient and will generally know nothing; they will be tiresome company, having the show of wisdom without the reality. (Plato, 2008 [360 BCE]: 69)

The language and forms of evidence may have changed, but the concern that communication technologies make us dumber is as old as writing. There is, as Lynn Spigel (2004: 140) put it, a "compulsion to repeat the same ideas, even as the society itself has noticeably changed." Reading books such as Marvin's *When Old Technologies Were New* (1988), *The Victorian Internet* (Standage, 1998), or Fischer's *America Calling* (1992) about the telephone's early days, the parallels between today's discourse, especially about the internet, and earlier rhetorics of technology are striking.

There are several variants of technological determinism. One, often linked to thinkers such as Canadian media theorist Marshall McLuhan, who coined the phrase "the medium is the message," is that technologies have characteristics that are transferred to those who use them. Claude Fischer calls this an "impact-imprint" perspective in which technologies change history by transferring "their essential qualities" to their users, imprinting themselves on users' individual and collective psyches (1992: 10). Fischer uses the example of Meyrowitz's influential book *No Sense of Place* (1985), which argued that, because physical and social spaces are separated through electronic media, people who use them lose their own sense of place. Arguments that the rapid-fire editing of current television film creates short attention spans, or that playing violent video games leads to violent behavior, represent other takes on this perspective. Seen this way, "a technology enters a society from outside and 'impacts' social life" (Fischer, 1992: 12).

Such direct effects of technology may be strongest when a technology is new because people do not yet understand it. Rather than "using" it, people may be "used by it" (Fischer, 1992: 12). Direct effects are also tied to thinking of technologies in a simplistic way: the more you use them, the more they use you, and the more you are influenced by them. For instance, many studies of internet use, some of which will be addressed in chapters 4 and 6, measure time spent online, divide people into heavy and light users, or users vs. non-users, and then correlate that measure with outcome variables such as loneliness or time spent with family. What a person was doing online is not addressed, collapsing such diverse activities as keeping in touch with one's mother, banking, researching political information, and looking at pornography into a single causal agent: The Internet.

In a milder form of technological determinism, media choice, technological features are seen as having direct consequences, but people are seen as making strategic, and usually rational, choices about which media they use for differing purposes. According to this perspective, "individuals will effectively employ media whose inherent characteristics are congruent with task demands" (Fulk, Steinfeld, Schmitz, & Power, 1987: 531). Change happens at an individual rather than societal level. By extension, this means that people are able to avoid technological influence by avoiding the technology. According to Lynne Markus (1994), however, the key issue is not which features have which effects. Instead "it is the degree to which the outcomes, whether positive or negative, are the inevitable results of technological characteristics, or whether they might be subject to other influences" (Markus, 1994: 122). Markus argues that technological determinism is ultimately an optimistic theory. If negative outcomes can be traced to technological causes, then they can be eliminated with better technology. It is also, however, a disempowering perspective that positions people as powerless to stop these changes unless they invent new, better, or different technologies or eschew technology altogether.

As the similarities amongst Socrates', Carr's and Alloway's articulation of new media's effect on wisdom suggest, deterministic rhetorics tend to be formulaic and hyperbolic (Turkle, 2004). Predictable negative stories are met with predictable positive alternatives in a familiar contradictory binary. In the 1920s, for instance, people anticipated that radio would "provide culture and education to the masses, eliminate politicians' ability to incite passions in a mob, bring people closer to government proceedings, and produce a national culture that would transcend regional and local jealousies" (Douglas, 2004 [1999]: 20). Now, Douglas continues, "we've been witness to all sorts of overheated and contradictory predictions about the Internet: it will re-create political and cultural communities in cyberspace; it will bring pornographers, stalkers, and credit-card scammers into our homes, corrupting our kids and ransacking our privacy."

American historian David Nye (1997) has done extensive research on how nineteenth-century Americans responded to new technologies of the time. As he summarized in a later article (2004), Americans could have used many narratives to make sense of new technology, but in practice usually used six, three *utopian*, envisioning a world improved by technology, and three *dystopian*, visions of a world made worse. In the utopian stories, technologies are seen as natural societal developments, improvements to daily life, or as forces that will transform reality for the better. Dystopian reactions emphasize fears of losing control, becoming dependent, and being unable to stop change. In the three dystopian rhetorics Nye identifies, technology may be seen as a way for elites to control the masses, as agents of doom, or as malevolent tricksters that promise positive change but in the end only make our lives more difficult. "The long history of popular culture's alternately fearful and euphoric representations of electronic communication," wrote Boddy (2004: 4), "suggests the continuing historical relevance of such ephemeral fantasies of pleasure and terror." Even in his dystopian article, Carr (2008) offered utopian visions, arguing that "the new technology did often have the effects [Socrates] feared," yet also that Socrates "couldn't foresee the many ways that writing and reading would serve to spread information, spur fresh ideas, and expand human knowledge (if not wisdom)."

Recurrent themes in the reception of new technology

We are surrounded by messages that treat media qualities as a cause of social consequences. In this section I identify common recurring themes regarding new media and social life that appear in popular media. In addition to previous theorists and cultural historians of technology, I make use of Janna Quitney Anderson's (2005) compilation of predictions and descriptions of the internet from newspapers, magazines, and other American sources from the early 1990s. I also use cartoons from the *New Yorker*, an influential and long-lived magazine that has been questioning our relationship to technology through humor since its inception in the 1920s, and letters from the two most popular American advice columns, "Ann Landers" and "Dear Abby." The *New Yorker* reached a sector of the American population – urban, educated, and affluent – most likely to be early adapters of the internet and earlier new technologies. "Ann Landers" and "Dear Abby" together reached as many as 110 million readers daily and, especially in the mid-1990s, could well have been the only mass messages about the role of the internet in intimate relationships that many people encountered. Though these sources might seem trivial, silly, or even gossipy, they should not be underestimated in their capacity to reflect pervasive cultural attitudes. Writers and editors design mass mediated messages in order to resonate with their audience's concerns. Their livelihood depends upon it. Though other kinds of messages, including scholarly reports such as we'll turn to in the remaining chapters, may be better sources of accurate information about new media effects, mass mediated messages are considerably more likely to influence how people think about new technology and, as we'll return to below, how they subsequently behave. The themes I'll consider in this section include issues of the authenticity of mediated communication and relationships, the quality of mediated interactions, the formation of new relationships, the effects of anonymity (honesty, deception, liberation, and the potential erasure of status), and the effects on existing close relationships (will they become closer, be replaced with mediated relationships, be forgone altogether). I postpone my discussion of the themes about children, specifically their status as potential victims and as dangerously empowered, until the section on social construction that follows.

Socrates' idea that writing provides "not truth, but only the semblance of truth" remains very much with us. At the core of most, if not all, of the rhetorics about mediated forms of personal connection is a persistent sense that mediated inter-action and the relationships sustained through it are not *real*. Many "fear that actual human connection has been irretrievably lost," although others hope "that communication technologies can promote human connectivity" (Sturken & Thomas, 2004: 3). In the telephone's early years, some worried it could sustain "only a sem-blance of 'real' relations" (Fischer, 1992: 224). The common use of the term "virtual" to describe online relationships and groups, and of the acronym "IRL" (in real life) to describe offline connections, are evidence of this deep-seated presumption.

People often question the *quality of mediated interactions*, believ-ing technological mediation takes away the social cues that provide rich meaning (a topic explored in depth in the next chapter). Walter Benjamin (2009 [1935]) famously argued that the "aura" of tangi-ble art provides much of its value, a value lessened in the age of mechanical reproduction. Replicating this concern, internet-critic Stoll (1995, cited in Anderson, 2005: 65), wrote that in comparison to letters, electronic interaction was cold: "The paper doesn't age, the signatures don't fade. Perhaps a future generation will save their romances on floppy disks [but] give me a shoebox of old letters."

Electronic messages are frequently portrayed as vacuous. A 2009 study by market research firm Pear Analytics, for instance, created a category called "pointless babble" into which they placed 40 percent of Twitter messages, echoing oft-heard complaints that mobile phones lead to empty conversation, sustained for the sake of interacting even when we have nothing to say (Twitter tweets are 40% "babble", 2009). The idea that new media cause pointless babble could also be seen in a 1927 *New Yorker* cartoon in which a luxuriantly robed, very made-up, clearly affluent, woman reclining on a couch said: "Hold the line a minute, dear – I'm trying to think what I have on my mind" (cartoon 2.1).

One of the hopes surrounding the internet is that it can *broaden our pool of potential relational partners* and lead to new relationships (a topic we will return to in chapter 5). For instance, this testimo-nial from "A Netizen in Chicago" appeared in "Ann Landers" in 1996:

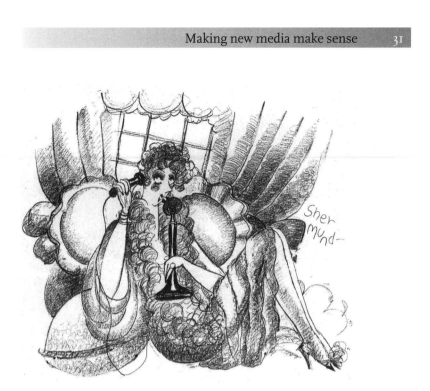

Cartoon 2.1: "Hold the line a minute dear. . .I'm trying to think what I have on my mind
© Barbara Shermund / Condé Nast

I met my girlfriend on the Net. She is Canadian. I live in Illinois. We have gotten together, face to face, only once, but over the last few months, we have gotten to know each other well. We have fallen in love. We have four meetings planned and call each other twice a week. We e-mail every night.

I also have made many friends on the Net. Most of us will never meet, but we offer our support when one of us is feeling blue and our accolades when things are going great.

On our news group alone, many friendships have developed. There have been four marriages so far, and several relationships are now in progress that will probably end up in marriage. None of us is hooked on the Net, but we do check frequently to see how our on-line pals are doing.

At the same time, many question whether relationships formed this way can ever be as real as those formed face to face. Cartoon 2.2, from 2006, plays off the befuddled faces of older parents against the smiling faces of a young – mediated – couple, showing

Cartoon 2.2: "We met online."
© David Sipress / Condé Nast

both the utopian hope for new relational opportunities and the wary uncertainty that surrounds them.

One reason for uncertainty in mediated environments is that, without visual and auditory social cues, people are not sure whether or not they can *trust* other people to be who they claim to be. This is the central problem of anonymity. Perhaps the best encapsulation of the binary between hope and dread that the anonymity of the internet provides is Peter Steiner's famous 1993 *New Yorker* cartoon of two dogs, one seated on a chair at the computer, the other sitting on the floor watching (cartoon 2.3). The computing dog explained to the other "On the Internet, nobody knows you're a dog," a caption which, writes Anderson (2005: 228), "will live forever as an online-culture touchstone." This cartoon has been reproduced in numerous scholarly articles and books, and become one of the most popular *New Yorker* cartoons ever, as indicated by its high rank on requested reprint and presentation rights. A Google search for its caption turns up more than 250,000 hits. Its transnational appeal

Cartoon 2.3: "On the Internet, nobody knows you're a dog."
© Peter Steiner / Condé Nast

can be seen in its appearance on the cover of an Estonian book about the internet (Institut Za Etnologiju I Folkloristiku, 2004). Although Steiner has said he didn't know what the cartoon was about when he drew it, *New Yorker* cartoon editor Robert Mankoff said it "perfectly predicted both the Internet's promise and its problems" (2004: 618). Whether this cartoon represents a dream or a nightmare depends on whether one is the dog or the fool unknowingly talking to the dog.

Of course, no one really expects house pets to go online and pretend to be people, but they often expect that sparse social cues will cause people to lie about themselves. As one man explained in a 1994 letter to "Ann Landers":

> Every woman on a computer line describes herself as Cindy Crawford, and
> every guy is Tom Cruise. Women lie about their marital status, weight, age
> and occupation. And get this, Ann, some women are actually guys.

Authentic self-representation is not always a simple question of true and false, as we will address in chapter 5. With its potential to liberate people from the constraints of their social context, people may also be seen as becoming *more honest* in mediated encounters. This advice column letter-writer admitted to Abby that she had presented a deceptive identity online, yet claimed the emotions and relationships predicated upon it were real:

> I am deeply in love with a man who is handsome, smart and loving. We are
> engaged and happy together. The problem? We met on the Internet. Abby,
> he thinks I am 26, but I'm not. Everything I've said to him has been a lie.
> I am really 12.

On a societal level, anonymity opens the possibility of *liberation* from the divisions that come about from seeing one another's race, age, gender, disabilities, and so on. Standage (1998) tells of an interracial relationship formed via telegraph without either party's knowledge of the other's racial identity. Early rhetoric about the internet often speculated that the reduction of social cues would lead to people valuing one another's contributions for their intrinsic worth rather than the speaker's status. The internet would lead to the world Martin Luther King Jr. dreamed of, in which people would be judged by the content of their character rather than the color of their skin. A now-legendary MCI advertisement that ran during the 1997 Superbowl described it like this: "There is no race, there are no genders, there is no age, there are no infirmities, there are only minds. Utopia? No, the Internet."

On the other hand, many people, especially in the middle and upper classes view social divisions as useful and necessary means of protecting themselves and their families from unwanted outside influences and dangers (Marvin, 1988; Spigel, 1992). For them, the specter of technological *erasure of social status information* is frightening. Communication technologies have long been represented as a source of stress for families, making it too easy for people to engage in "irregular courtship" with people outside the community (Marvin, 1988: 73). The telephone was feared for its potential to enable the "wrong kinds" of sociability across age, class, and racial lines (Fischer, 1992: 225). When the telephone was new, articles criticized ordinary people who called New York City's mayor regularly, simply because they now could. Those placing the calls might have understood this as a utopian outcome of the technology – allowing them greater access to those of significantly higher status and greater ability to participate in governance – but, for the mayor and other members of the elite, it demonstrated an intrusive threat. Furthermore, even when people themselves do not enter the sanctuary of the privileged, their communication artifacts might. The phonograph and radio were often viewed as corrupting because they raised the specter of interracial interaction (and sex!) by bringing ragtime and jazz music written and performed by black artists into affluent white homes (Douglas, 2004 [1999]).

Building new online relationships has been both touted and decried as a way for a person to "assemble his or her own electronic neighborhood" (Dertouzos, 1991 in Anderson, 2005: 49). Though some, such as Dertouzos, see this as a perk, others worry that rather than lessening differences in social class, social divides will be reproduced or increased by technology. "The superhighway may connect us more to other people of similar interests and beliefs," worried Brown in the *Seattle Post-Intelligencer* (1995, cited in Anderson, 2005: 64), "But we'll have less communication with those who are different. Socially we may find ourselves returning to a form of tribalism, as we separate ourselves along group lines – racial, ethnic, ideological – choosing access to only the information that speaks to our identities and beliefs."

Technologically deterministic rhetorics also frame new communication media as improving and damaging the close personal relationships people sustain face to face. The telephone was seen as a means to bring people closer together, build communities, and decrease loneliness (de Sola Pool, 1977; Fischer, 1992). Electricity was going to decrease the divorce rate since it would make domestic chores easier to do and lessen the conflict they created (Marvin, 1988). The automobile spawned dreams of family togetherness

(Fischer, 1992), as seen in the recurrent motif of the car-based family vacation. Early ads for the radio and phonograph often showed happy families where clean children looked approvingly at their parents as they gathered around the technology in their living rooms. As Spigel (1992: 3) shows in her analysis of popular communication during television's early years, the television "was depicted as a panacea for the broken homes and hearts of wartime life . . . shown to restore faith in family togetherness . . . however . . . equally dystopian discourses warned of television's devastating effects on family relationships and the efficient functioning household."

In the context of contemporary digital media, the hope remains that new communication technologies will *bring families and loved ones together*. Today, we hear of people staying in touch with their children through Facebook, or using mobile "family plans" to keep the family in continuous contact. A 1995 article in *Wired* predicted that the family would rise to the top of a new communication hierarchy: "Every family will have its own mailing list carrying contributions from its members. . . . I sense that the rules will be something like this: friends over strangers; family over friends; and within those categories, the geographically or chronologically close over the distant" (Hapgood, 1995, cited in Anderson, 2005: 64).

The dystopian alternative is usually articulated as a fear that new media will take people away from their intimate relationships, as they *substitute* mediated relationships or even media use itself for face to face engagement. Fischer (1992) described early twentieth-century concerns that the telephone would replace visiting. The fear of substituting mediated for meaningful relationships also occurred around television. A 1962 *New Yorker* cartoon, for instance, showed a husband and wife seated at the dinner table, his face buried in a newspaper (cartoon 2.4). The wife watched a television depicting a couple sharing a romantic dinner. The image on the screen simulated intimacy while media old (newspaper) and new (television) kept the spouses from connecting with each other.

A common motif in stories of digital media damaging relationships is the "cyberaffair." One of the most recurrent metaphors advice columns used to describe the internet during its early

Cartoon 2.4
© Leonard Dave / Condé Nast

American diffusion was "homewrecker." Published letters and replies repeatedly described men and women who, upon getting access to the internet, found a new love (or pornography), and ruined their marriage. A 1995 letter to "Ann Landers" begged Ann to warn readers about "an insidious monster about to pounce on the American people. It will destroy more marriages and lives than anything the world has ever known. It's called the Internet." Ann Landers cast the phenomenon as rampant, writing in 1998, "My mail tells me that the Internet may become the principal home-wrecker of the next century."

In addition to ruining close relationships, the internet and other new media are frequently depicted as causing *social isolation*. In the *Wall Street Journal*, Hays speculated that "[c]onnecting with one and all in the electronic ether could leave people more discon-nected than ever before, as the necessity of face to face contact diminishes. If a troubled or shy office worker easily finds solace and approval on the networks, will she be less inclined to seek out friends on the job?" (1993, cited in Anderson, 2005: 96). Writers to "Ann Landers" and "Dear Abby" in the late 1990s frequently described internet users as "junkies" who get "addicted" to the internet, destroying their close relationships. One wrote:

> My husband of 22 years has become a recluse. He refuses social invitations, has quit attending our children's activities and lies to me about the amount of time he spends surfing the 'Net. Like an alcoholic, he apologizes and promises to do better, but once the computer clicks on, he sits there, transfixed, until the wee hours of the morning. (1998)

"People are not going to want to leave their homes when they can have more fun in cyberspace," warned futurist Faith Popcorn in the *London Independent* (Anderson, 2005: 67–8). In *US News & World Report*, Neal Postman offered a futuristic scenario that summarized the dystopian fears concisely:

> Public life will have disappeared because we did not see, in time to reverse the process, that our dazzling technologies were privatizing almost all social activities. . . . We replaced meeting friends with the video telephone and electronic mail . . . We became afraid of real people and eventually forgot how to behave in public places, which had become occupied almost entirely by criminals. The rest of us had no need to be with each other. (1993, cited in Anderson, 2005: 96)

To summarize, technologically determinist rhetorics of digital media, like those of previous communication technologies, often focus on the authenticity of identity and the well-being of "real" relationships. Utopian rhetorics emphasize the happy prospect that technology will liberate true selves from the constraints of geography and the shackles of marginalized social identities and empower them to enrich their offline relationships and engage in new online relationships. These visions are pitted against tangled dystopian scenarios of deception, tribalism, and the erasure of social class distinctions. These perpetuate fears that communication technologies will take us farther apart from one another, leading us to cocoon in highly selective groups of like others, embracing machines instead of people. These rhetorics are predictable, and tell us as much – if not more – about society than they tell us about technologies. They point to our deep need to trust, connect with, and protect one another and ourselves, and the perpetual struggles these needs engender.

Social construction of technology

People have the power

In the examples I have just discussed, and the historical trends they represent, technology is positioned as causing us and our social lives to change. Determinism views technology as arising independent of social contexts and then affecting them. Other perspectives share concern about the same issues, but do not grant technology as much causal agency. The Social Construction of Technology (SCOT) perspective focuses on how technologies arise from social processes. SCOT proponents view technologically deterministic perspectives as "inadequate as explanations and dangerously misleading [because] human beings, not machines, are the agents of change, as men and women introduce new systems of machines that alter their life world" (Nye, 1997: 180). One focus of social constructivism is how social forces influence the invention of new technologies (e.g. Bijker & Law, 1992; Bijker, Hughes, & Pinch 1987). From a SCOT perspective, inventors are embedded in social contexts that make it feasible to use a garage to create a personal computer or a bicycle repair shop to invent an airplane. The choices that designers and developers make as they develop technology are seen as dependent on their social contexts which are, in turn, shaped in part by communication. In the contemporary context, one might look at the female avatars available in online games, characters that are almost uniformly shaped like pornographic fantasy figures, and posit that this is related to their having been designed by people – primarily male – who are embedded in a patriarchal culture that views women as sex objects and thinks of their primary audience as men and boys.

Furthermore, SCOT theorists see technological development as influenced by many factors beyond the inventors. Investors – both private and governmental – have priorities that shape which technologies are deemed worthy of pursuit and given the resources to enable their success. Competitors drive development in different directions, as seen, for instance, in Microsoft turning from a DOS interface to Windows in emulation of Apple's graphic operating system, or Facebook's efforts to capitalize on the success of Twitter with revisions of its own site. Government agencies may shape technological development with their dispersion of grant monies. Furthermore, users shape development, especially, as Fischer (1992) notes, when they are organized. These differing sources of influence do not always agree. Indeed, they are often in conflict with one another, and the shape of any given technology is often a matter of compromise.

SCOT proponents also focus on what happens during technological adoption, arguing that a wide range of social, economic, governmental, and cultural factors influence how people take up and use media. In his study of the adoption of the telephone, Fischer (1992: 269) argued for a "user perspective." "Users," he wrote, "try to put a new technology to their own ends, which can lead to paradoxical outcomes not easily deducible from the straightforward logic of the technology." Lister, Dovey, Giddings, Grant, and Kelly (2003: 81) draw on media theorist Raymond Williams to argue that "whatever the original intention to develop a technology might be, subsequently other social groups, with different interests or needs, adapt, modify or subvert the uses to which any particular technology is put." Communication about technology, as seen in the messages discussed above, is one important force in these processes. The telegraph, radio, refrigerator, and internet are all technologies whose unexpected uses became their most common (Nye, 2004). The internet, conceived as a military back-up system, exemplifies technology re-envisioned and transformed by its users.

Though it's important to understand the power users have, it's easy to put too much influence on individuals, when, as Fischer (1992) notes, there are other social structures at play, including access, availability, price, and marketing. Texting is an interesting example of this. It used to be that when I mentioned using mobile phones to send text messages, most of my college students – almost all of whom had mobile phones in their pockets – stared blankly. They'd never heard of such a thing, despite the fact that this had become a major use of mobile phones in other countries in Asia and Europe years earlier. Around 2005, pricing plans on US cell phone contracts changed to make texting inexpensive. Now my students all use this feature of the phone. They no longer stare blankly. Indeed, some of them are too busy texting under their desks to register what I am saying.

The social influence model proposed by Janet Fulk (1993) draws attention to the influence of peers on individuals' perceptions and subsequent uses of media. In her work on adoption of new media (specifically email) in an organizational context, she found that the perspectives of peers, especially "attractive" peers – those who are friends as well as good colleagues – were strong influences on individuals' attitudes towards email. In a study of attitudes towards mobile phones in the Midwestern United States, Campbell and Russo (2003) also showed that attitudes towards behaviors such as whether or not one should turn off the mobile in a restaurant were shaped by the attitudes of peers. As people discuss new media, and as those media are represented in other media such as television, print, and film, devices themselves come to carry social meaning (so that some phones look cool, and others look dorky). Media are also discursively associated with genders, so that computers are often cast as male, and telephones as female (Rakow, 1992; Hijazi-Omari & Ribak, 2008).

Moral panic

As we saw in our discussion of technological determinism, new media often stir up fears of moral decline. These fears, which take form in dystopian rhetorics, can lead to important policy decisions at personal, household, governmental, and design levels. In other words, the communication about the technologies becomes more important than the technologies in shaping the uses and effects of new media. Such rhetorics often focus on the well-being of children, and especially on the well-being of teenage girls. Concerns about protecting children seem to arise almost instantaneously in the wake of any new communication medium. Children are often seen as innocents who can be corrupted, damaged, and permanently transformed by technology in ways that parents are powerless to prevent (Marvin, 2004; Sturken & Thomas, 2004). "The relationship of children and media culture, and the larger social context in which this relationship is forged," wrote Marvin (2004: 283), "is constantly debated and rehashed in the popular press and in public discourse." The automobile led to fears that teenagers would isolate themselves from their families (Fischer, 1992). Among the media that have been charged with causing children to mature too soon and/or become juvenile delinquents are books, movies, comic books, and television (Fang, 2008). In American history, dime novels, so popular in the mid 1800s, spawned concern about the intellectual development of their readers, potential increases in anti-social behavior, and criminality, but also fostered hopes that the new medium could be used for enlightenment (Fang, 2008).

These days, children are seen as likely to be exposed to (or, worse yet, exploited for) pornography and sexual encounters. The most prominent examples of this in the discourse around the internet concern sexual predation. To hear much of the public representation of the internet is to imagine a world in which sexual crimes are reaching new heights as unwitting innocents are drawn into deceptive relationships that end in molestation, abduction, and even death. Adult men do sometimes use the internet to lure girls into inappropriate relationships. This is surely awful, but it is very unusual. When adult men and underage girls do meet through the internet for sexual encounters, it is usually consensual and honest, if morally dubious (Cassell & Cramer, 2007). Cassell and Cramer's close analysis of US federal crime report data regarding crimes against children shows that crimes against people 12–17 years old fell between 46 percent and 69 percent after 1993–1995, despite the fact that millions of young people integrated the internet into their lives in that time frame. Sexual predation between strangers remains extremely infrequent relative to sexual predation within existing relationships, and assaults between those who met online are but a tiny proportion of stranger crimes (Internet Safety Technical Task Force, 2008).

What has happened around the fear of sexual predation is a classic case of a "moral panic" in which anxieties over uncontrollable social forces become the focus of efforts to understand a new cultural trend (Cohen, 1972). Panics displace our anxieties over something more important onto the technology, perhaps because they are too difficult or threatening to face directly (D. Thomas, 2004). One could just as easily argue that the internet has protected teens by keeping them home. Sexual predation is terrible, but if your goal is to reduce sexual crimes against children or women, the internet is the wrong place to focus. It is, however, a much easier target than our own marriages, homes, neighborhoods, places of worship, and schools, where most crimes against children and women occur (Internet Safety Technical Task Force, 2008).

The flip side to children's abilities to do new things outside parental supervision through technology is that children are often seen not just as endangered, but as dangerous. Their knowledge of technology is often seen as being greater than that of adults (although Livingstone, 2008, presented evidence that children don't always feel this way). Children do develop skills and use technologies in ways that limit how much parents and others can control them (Banet-Weiser, 2004; Marvin, 2004), and which can even harm parents.

The phenomenon of "sexting" in which young people share naked photographs of themselves with each other via their mobile phones is a novel twist on this, combining the fear of children's sexuality and its potential negative consequences with the fear of children's empowerment. Adults are "afraid of children, afraid of new technologies, and, most important, afraid of the usage by and reaction of children to digital media and new technologies" (Banet-Weiser, 2004: 286).

Fears about children can be understood as arising from parents' fear of losing control over them, a problem inherent in child rearing, regardless of whatever technologies may or may not be present. Since fear is often displaced onto seemingly more-manageable technology, parents and governments often try to protect children by implementing surveillance systems, legislating policy limitations on children's access to technology, and even creating new technologies to limit children's interaction with technology (Marvin, 2004: 281). Displacing our anxieties about children's safety onto the internet and mobile phones makes our fear more manageable, but does little to protect children, and may keep them from realizing the benefits new technologies can offer them (Cassell & Cramer, 2007).

In sum, social constructivism provides a polar alternative to technological determinism. Rather than viewing social change as a consequence of new media, it views new technologies and their uses as consequences of social factors. From this perspective, the utopian and dystopian rhetorics I discussed above tell us little about the technology, but do provide insight into how technologies come to be and how they come to be understood and used. The example of moral panics shows how deterministic rhetorics can give rise to understandings of technology and to policy decisions which in turn shape the uses and consequences of those media, though not always as intended.

Social shaping of technology

The truth, as is so often the case, lies somewhere in between. If technological determinism locates cause with the technology, and social constructivism locates cause with people, a third perspective, sometimes called social shaping, emphasizes a middle ground. From this perspective, the consequences of technologies arise from a mix of "affordances" – the social capabilities technological qualities enable – and the unexpected and emergent ways that people make use of those affordances. Katz and Aakhus (2002) speak of technologies having "logics" or "apparatgeists" that influence but do not determine use. "Machines," wrote Douglas (2004 [1999]: 21) "do not make history by themselves. But some kinds of machines help make different kinds of histories and different kinds of people than others." Machines "can and do accelerate certain trends, magnify cultural weaknesses, and fortify certain social structures while eroding others" (Douglas, 1999: 20).

People, technologies, and institutions all have power to influence the development and subsequent use of technology. They are "interrelated nodes in constantly changing sociotechnical networks, which constitute the forms and uses of technology differently in different times and places for different groups" (Lievrouw, 2006: 250). From the social shaping perspective, we need to consider how societal circumstances give rise to technologies, what specific possibilities and constraints technologies offer, and actual practices of use as those possibilities and constraints are taken up, rejected, and reworked in everyday life.

Domestication of technology

The fact that we no longer engage in either utopian or dystopian discourses about the landline telephone or, for that matter, the alphabet is evidence of how successfully earlier technologies have been *domesticated*. What once seemed marvelous and strange, capable of creating greatness and horror, is now so ordinary as to be invisible. Life without them can become unimaginable (my son once asked how we used the internet before computers were invented). British and Norwegian media and technology studies in the 1990s developed the "domestication" approach to technology in order to continue where the social shaping of technology leaves off (Haddon, 2006). This approach concurs with social shaping in seeing both technology and society as influences in the consequences of new media, but it is particularly concerned with the processes at play as new technologies move from being fringe (wild) objects to everyday (tame) objects embedded deeply in the practices of daily life. Early domestication work showed that, by the time most users encounter technologies, they are already laden with the social meanings given them by advertisement, design, and the kinds of rhetorics we have been discussing. Nonetheless, "both households and individuals then invest them with their own personal meanings and significance" (Haddon, 2006: 196). The process of domestication plays out at societal levels, but also in daily interactions as people figure out where to place devices, and, more importantly, who gets to use them for what and who doesn't (Silverstone, Hirsch, & Morley, 1992).

As technologies are integrated into everyday life, they come to be seen as offering a nuanced mix of both positive and negative implications. Syntopian perspectives (Katz & Rice, 2002) view new technologies as simultaneously enabling and disabling. The extremes may persist, but in between we use communication to negotiate a vast realm of detail, contradiction, and complexity. In closing this chapter, I want to consider how we move from a period where new technologies are threatening or exciting to one in which they are ordinary and barely worthy of remark. The advice columns I drew on above serve as a remarkable microcosm through which to see domestication of the internet in action.

In early letters, particularly those prior to 2000, there was a very clear norm that the internet was dangerous. Internet users were often described as junkies, addicts, recluses or, at best and on average "fairly decent people" (as Ann Landers wrote in 1994). Both columns had readers who were having different experiences, however, and the columns provided a venue in which those having good experiences were able to resist the negative image of the technology being constructed in others' letters and in Ann and Abby's responses. A Netizen in Chicago's 1996 letter (seen above) explaining all the positive relationships he had built online is one example. Similar letters from many others singing the praises of the internet poured in. The mail, wrote Landers in 1996, was "staggering, and most of the readers agree."

Letter writers defended the internet against dystopian visions in many ways. One was through the use of metaphor, comparing the internet to fire, parks, knives, and, in one letter (which I swear I did not write) the telephone, as seen in these 1996 examples:

> Saying the Net is destructive because it can be used incorrectly is like saying humankind would be better off without fire because it can be dangerous.

> Get a clue, Ann. Condemning the Internet because some people meet scoundrels on-line is like condemning parks because some pedophile exposed himself to children in a park.

> The problem with people and the Internet is not the Internet but what people do with it. The same is true of a knife. I was under the knife having lifesaving surgery the same day someone across town was murdered by one.

> Wary of the Internet, Ann? I'll bet if you had been around in the 1880s, you'd have been suspicious of the telephone because it could be used for "nefarious purposes." Anything new needs time to be accepted.

As seen in this comparison between the telephone and the internet, letter writers who defended the internet often took a social constructivist perspective on the relationship between technology and society. Some explicitly challenged Ann's, Abby's, and other letter writers' construction of the technology's status as cause rather than symptom:

> You have said that the Internet has disrupted relationships between couples and destroyed marriages. That is not the fault of the Internet. Those relationships were already in trouble. (1996)

> People who stay up all night on their computers don't have an Internet problem. They have an addiction problem. (1997)

Others took a social shaping stance in which the internet was positioned as a contributing factor when combined with other problems:

> Our 19-year marriage had been rather rocky, what with career problems, financial woes, children and other pressures. Then, my husband, "Ron," discovered the chat lines. (1996)

> Mark my words, Ann, mid-life and the Internet are an explosive combination that spells double trouble. (1996)

By the end of the 1990s, both columnists took a social shaping perspective on the relationship between the internet and social problems. The technology was seen as enabling some new possibilities for trouble, but the troubles belonged firmly to the people perpetrating the behaviors. Ann Landers eventually wrote that the internet posed a threat to "sterile" marriages (1996), but was not "a 'killer of marriages' any more than TV was when it first entered our living rooms" (1998). "Get out the wet noodle," Landers wrote in her inimitable style, "My readers have convinced me that the Internet, when used properly, has a lot more to offer than I thought" (1999).

Once this more nuanced understanding had been reached, the

internet continued to appear as a character in letters to advice columns, but the tone changed considerably. For instance, the writer of a 2004 letter about a fiancé who had placed a personal ad on an online dating site was told that her fiancé "does not understand the responsibilities and obligations of marriage" and that "he might run off with the neighbor's wife." In contrast to earlier replies in which Ann and Abby bemoaned an "epidemic" of home-wrecking due to the internet, the internet was not even mentioned in this response. By 2004, it had become almost invisible.

That the internet has been largely domesticated does not mean that all anxieties surrounding it have been resolved. Digital media still appear in advice columns, in *New Yorker* cartoons, in all other popular media, and in everyday conversations. Just as one form of mediated communication becomes domesticated (email may be a strong contender for this status), another arises with some new twist to confuse us. The social concerns that we voice when we discuss technology are concerns we would have even if there were no technology around. They are questions of what it means to be truly yourself, to have meaningful relationships with others, and to be situated in a world of others who are very different from the people by whom we were raised.

Social shaping and domestication differ in where they put the emphasis on the social processes involved in making sense of the technology–society relationship, but agree that the direction of influence is, at the very least, two-way. Rather than being deterministic, they see the consequences of technology on social life as *emergent*. Even if we knew all the factors that influence us at the start (an impossible feat), we would not be able to precisely predict the social interactions, formations, and changes that result from their ongoing interplay as people use technologies in specific situations.

This book adheres to social shaping and domestication perspectives, arguing that, in order to connect digital media to social consequences, we need to understand both features of technology and the practices that influence and emerge around technology, including the role of technological rhetorics in those practices. If you turn the page expecting to find simple answers to the question of what computers and mobile phones do to our personal connections, you will be disappointed. They do many things, and which ones they do to which people depends on many forces, only some of which are predictable. As the chapters that follow will show, sometimes these media are used in ways that are predictable given media affordances (people call to say they are running late more because they have mobile phones on hand through which to do it), surprising (the American social network site Orkut came quickly to be dominated by Brazilians and later Indians, who appropriated it as their primary site), disruptive (people form close relationships before meeting in person), and affirming (people use the mobile phone to increase family cohesion). The complexity of the social shaping and domestication perspectives does not mean we should throw up our hands and despair of gaining any insight. We should, however, always be wary of simple explanations.

3

Communication in digital spaces

If asked to share general thoughts about communicating face to face, on the telephone, and on the internet, many people' are likely to say something like this:

> Face to face is much more personal; phone is personal as well, but not as intimate as face to face. The internet is the least personal but it's always available.

> Face to face: I enjoy the best. I like to see facial reactions, etc. Phone: nice to hear their voice, but wish I could see their reactions. Internet: like it, but can't get a true sense of the person.

> I am more apt to be more affectionate and personable face to face. Over the phone, I can try to convey them, but they don't work as well. The internet is much too impersonal to communicate feelings.

> Internet would definitely be the least personal, followed by the phone (which at least has the vocal satisfaction) and the most personal would be face to face.

These responses to a survey I conducted in 2002 framed the comparison in terms of the extent to which nonverbal social cues ("hear their voice," "see their reactions," "vocal satisfaction") affected the perceived intimacy of each medium.

In the first chapter, we saw that a medium's ability to convey social cues about interactants and context is an essential component of its communicative possibilities and constraints. In the last chapter, we saw historical and contemporary visions, both hopeful and fearful, about how limited social cues may affect people, relationships, and social hierarchies. Media with fewer social cues often trigger hopes that people will become more equal and more valued for their minds than their social identities, but also raise fears that interactions, identities, and relationships will become increasingly shallow, untrustworthy, and inadequate.

This chapter asks what happens to communication itself – the messages people exchange – when it's digitally mediated. We begin by examining the perspective seen in the quotes at the start of this chapter, that mediation is impoverishment. We'll look closely at the practice of "flaming," or extremely argumentative communication, as a test case for considering the extent to which a lack of cues can be considered a cause of how people behave. Having established that there's more going on than can be explained by a mere shortage of nonverbal cues, we'll see how people inject sociability into mediated communication, showing emotion, expressing closeness and availability, having fun, and building new social structures. I'll argue that mediated interaction should be seen as a new and eclectic mixed modality that combines elements of face to face communication with elements of writing, rather than as a diminished form of embodied interaction. In the closing section of the chapter, we'll consider how messages online are influenced by and potentially reshape social identities that transcend media, including gender and culture.

Mediation as impoverishment

Reduced social cues

The quotes that opened this chapter demonstrate a formulaic tendency to think about media in ranked order and to position the one that seems to offer the widest range of verbal and nonverbal social cues on top and the one seeming to offer the least on the bottom. As we saw in the last chapter, this is in keeping with popular discourses throughout history and may well resonate with your own intuitions. It is also in keeping with early research approaches that conceptualized face to face conversations as the norm against which other kinds of communication could be compared. From this point of view, mediated communication is seen as a diminished form of face to face conversation. Taking embodied co-present communication as the norm, early research often saw the telephone and internet as lesser versions of the real thing, inherently less intimate, and, therefore, less suited to personal connections.

The first research comparing mediated interaction to face to face communication began in the 1970s. At this time, audioconferencing, videoconferencing, and networked computer systems were being installed in large organizational contexts. Research was driven by managerial concerns about when to choose each medium. Put simply, both managers and scholars wanted to know when they could hold a teleconference and when they would need to get employees together face to face. The first two theories of media choice, Social Presence Theory (Short, Williams, & Christie, 1976) and Media Richness Theory (Daft & Lengel, 1984), both tried to match media capabilities, defined as their ability to transmit social cues, with task demands.

Short and his collaborators (1976) were interested in how different degrees of social cues invoked differing senses of communication with an authentic person during synchronous interaction. They defined social presence as "the degree of salience of the other person in the interaction and the consequent salience (and perceived intimacy and immediacy) of the interpersonal relationships" (1976: 65). Thurlow, Lengel, and Tomic (2004: 48) describe social presence as the "level of interpersonal contact and feelings of intimacy experienced in communication."

Social presence is a psychological phenomenon regarding how interactants perceive one another, not a feature of a medium. However, the perception of social presence was attributed to the nonverbal cues enabled or disabled by mediation. Important nonverbal cues include facial expression, direction of gaze, posture, dress, physical appearance, proximity, and bodily orientation. In body to body communication, these nonverbal cues serve important functions (e.g. Wiemann & Knapp, 1975). For example, looking at someone, turning your torso towards them, nodding your head, and using fillers such as "uh huh" are all ways that we demonstrate attentiveness (e.g. Goodwin, 1981). We rely on gestures to keep our audience tuned in and to illustrate our words. Nonverbal "emblems" such as the American thumbs-up gesture have direct verbal translations (in this case, "yes," "good job," or "can I have a ride?" although the same gesture might directly translate into something far more provocative elsewhere). Facial expressions including smiles, furrowed brows, and clenched teeth convey inter-personal attitudes of liking and aversion, as well as cognitive states such as confusion and understanding (e.g. Andersen & Guerrero, 1998). Given the importance of these nonverbal cues in coordi-nating interaction and conveying meaning, especially emotional meaning, it makes sense that people question whether mediated communication can successfully serve social functions.

Social Presence theorists argued that if you knew which social cues served which functions in conversation, and you knew which media transmitted which cues, you would be able to predict how much social presence people using a medium would experience. In particular, they expected that groups completing tasks that involved maintaining personal relationships would require media that con-veyed more social cues than groups performing tasks in which people were primarily acting out social roles. In experiments, they found that people experienced more sense of social contact in face to face encounters than in videoconferences (Short et al., 1976). As Fulk and Collins-Jarvis (2001: 629) summarize, in several related studies people were found to perceive the least social presence of all in audio meetings "which are seen as less personal, less effec-tive for getting to know someone, and communicate less affective content than face to face."

Social Presence Theory focuses on the perception of others as real and present. Media Richness Theory, developed by Daft and Lengel (1984), is closely related, but focuses directly on the medium. Daft and Lengel (1984) defined a medium's rich-ness as its information-carrying capacity, which they based on four criteria: the speed of feedback, the ability to communicate multiple cues, its use of natural language rather than numbers, and its ability to readily convey feelings and emotions (a factor I find conceptually difficult to tease apart from the conveyance of multiple cues). Media Richness scholars compared rich and lean media for their suitability for solving tasks differing in equivocality and uncertainty. In contrast to Social Presence researchers, most

Media Richness research focused on asynchronous communication (Fulk & Collins-Jarvis, 2001). The expectation was that tasks high in uncertainty with many possible answers, such as resolving personnel issues, would work better in rich media, while unequivocal tasks like telling someone you're running late would be best served by lean media (Daft & Lengel, 1984).

These two theories – developed in a time when all online interaction was text-only – and related work from around that time can be considered "cues filtered out" approaches (Walther, Anderson, & Park, 1994). In their simplest forms, cues filtered out approaches assume that, to varying degrees, mediated communication is lean and therefore impedes people's ability to handle interpersonal dimensions of interaction. Because computer-mediated interactants are unable to see, hear, and feel one another, they can't use the usual cues conveyed by appearance, nonverbal signals, and features of the physical context. Mediated communication may be better than face to face interaction for some tasks, but for those involving personal identities and feelings, mediation was depicted as inherently inferior (Fulk & Collins-Jarvis, 2001).

Cues filtered out studies examining how reduced cues affected social qualities of communication (e.g. Baron, 1984; Kiesler, Siegel, & McGuire, 1984) had several expectations, which resonate with much of the public discourse we saw in the last chapter. First, mediation would make it more difficult to maintain conversational alignment and mutual understanding. Messages would be harder to coordinate. This would mean that communicators would have to work harder to achieve their desired impact and be understood.

Second, because social identity cues would not be apparent, interactants would gain greater anonymity. Their gender, race, rank, physical appearance, and other features of public identity are not immediately evident. As a result, people would be "depersonalized," losing their sense of self and other. This impersonal environment would make these media inherently less sociable and inappropriate for affective bonds. On the other hand, anonymity was also expected to result in a redistribution of social power, echoing the visions of blurred social status seen in the last chapter. With the cues to hierarchy (e.g. age, attire, seating arrangement) missing, participation would become more evenly distributed across group members. This egalitarian balance would make it difficult for people to dominate and impose their views on others (Baron, 1984; Walther, 1992). For those seeking speedy task resolution, the plurality of voices could mean tasks would take longer to accomplish. When everyone voices opinions, it often takes longer to reach a decision, complete a task, or achieve consensus (Sproull & Kiesler, 1991).

Cues filtered out researchers also expected that the lack of social cues would result in contexts without social norms to guide behavior (Kiesler et al., 1984; Rice, 1984, 1989; Sproull & Kiesler, 1991). Where face to face communication is regulated by implicit norms made apparent in the social context (for example, that this is a formal situation and it would not be appropriate to stand up enraged and start swearing), computer-mediated discourse was seen as a social vacuum in which anything went. Among other predictions, this was expected to lead to less social and emotional (socioemotional) communication and, somewhat paradoxically, more negatively loaded emotional communication. Instead of following the social norms mandating politeness and civility, rendered anonymous by the absence of social cues we would be meaner to one another than we would ever be in person.

These theories made enduring contributions to our understandings of communication media. The concepts of social presence and media richness continue to influence the ways scholars think about the consequences of mediation for interaction, and have become important pieces of later analytic frameworks. Furthermore, their predictions about task accomplishment have held up well in research and in practice. However, their expectations about social interaction turned out to be problematic at best and sometimes downright wrong. Certainly some people do become aggressive sometimes under some circumstances, a phenomenon to which we'll return below, but people also build warm loving relationships and provide one another with all kinds of social support, phenomena for which these approaches failed to account. Despite their contributions, they fall short as ways to describe and explain mediated communication's social consequences.

One reason for this is that scholars tended to use experimental research strategies that were unrealistic, usually involving small groups in short-term one-shot interactions in which they were supposed to accomplish an assigned task (Rafaeli & Sudweeks, 1997; Walther et al., 1994). Furthermore, their research findings, and findings from other lines of research, provide grounds for empirical criticisms. Lab studies did find statistically significant differences between face to face and computer-mediated communication, but the differences were very small (Walther et al., 1994).

More importantly, the few field studies where researchers spent time in naturally occurring contexts in which computer systems were already being used demonstrated that socioemotional communication not only existed, but was more likely to be prosocial than antisocial (Hiltz & Turoff, 1978). The social cues reported in early field studies included typographical art, salutations, the degree of formality of language, paralanguage, communication styles, and message headers (Hiltz & Turoff, 1978; Lea, O'Shea, Fung, & Spears, 1992). In a content analysis of transcripts from a professionally oriented CompuServe forum, Rice and Love (1987) found that socioemotional content (defined as showing solidarity, tension relief, agreement, antagonism, tension, and disagreement) constituted around 30 percent of messages, and was mostly positive.

Cues filtered out approaches can also be criticized for how they conceptualize the forces at play. The very definition of media richness distinguishes the conveyance of emotion from the ability to convey social cues, though they are profoundly interrelated. Many studies counted all emotional expression as evidence of disinhibition (Lea et al., 1992), with the result that friendly asides were seen as evidence of a norm-free medium. In fact, as we'll discuss in the next chapter, over time, mediated groups develop strong communicative norms that guide behavior. Furthermore, positive consequences of disinhibition such as increased honesty and self-disclosure, of the sort we will see in chapter 5, were also overlooked or assumed to be negative.

The perspective that mediated communication is a diminished form of face to face communication ignores many other factors that affect mediated communication, such as people's familiarity with the technology, whether they know one another already and what sort of relationship they have, whether they anticipate meeting or seeing one another again, their expectations and motivations for interacting, and the social contexts in which interactions are embedded. But, more significantly, it sells people short, failing to recognize the extent to which we are driven to maximize our communication satisfaction and interaction. This "communication imperative" (Walther, 1994) pushes us to use new media for interpersonal purposes and to come up with creative ways to work around barriers, rather than submitting ourselves to a context- and emotion-free communication experience.

The example of antagonism

Despite its problems, as the comments with which I opened this chapter and some of the technological rhetorics seen in the last chapter demonstrate, the cues filtered out approach still rings true for many. I would be the first to insist that nothing can replace a warm hug. But even if we accept that face to face communication provides a kind of social connection that simply cannot be attained with mediation, it does not follow that mediated communication, even in lean media, is emotionally or socially impoverished, or that social context cannot be achieved.

In chapter 2, I argued that our best shot at understanding the social consequences of mediated communication is a social shaping stance that recognizes both technological and social influences on behaviors. Research on flaming helps to illustrate how both qualities of the medium and emergent group norms influence online group behavior. Walther et al. (1994) defined flaming as messages that include swearing, insults, name calling, negative affect, and typographic energy. Flaming is exactly the kind of behavior that cues filtered out approaches predict and it is widely perceived as both common and unpleasant online. If cues filtered out theory were going to be able to fully explain one thing about social interaction, this should be it.

This flame from the Usenet newsgroup rec.arts.startrek.current from 1993 remains one of my favorites for its ability to illustrate how virulent, petty, mean, and yet entertaining flames can be:

>>Just fine by me. Personally I'd like to involve Lursa and her sister (the
>> Klingons) too. Now THAT would be a fun date.
>>
>> - Jim Hyde

> Will you stupid jerks get a real life. Everyone with half a brain or
> more know that a human and a Kligon can not mate. The Klingon mating
> procedure would kill any human (except one with a brain like you).
> Stay of the net stoopid!

Oh really. Hmmmm. And I suppose Alexander and his mom are just clones or something? If you recall, she is half human, and Alexander is 1/4. Romulans don't seem any more sturdy than humans, and we saw hybrids there as well.

Looks like I'm not the one with half a brain. Check your facts before you become the net.nazi next time pal. This isn't just a forum for us to all bow down and worship your opinion you know. You might also do well for yourself to learn how to spell, stooopid.

- Jim Hyde

These messages occur predictably in online group interactions and often lead to "flame wars" in which flames are met with hostile retorts. The hostilities escalate, drawing in more participants. Other participants chime in urging the original participants to move the discussion off-list or ignore the hostilities. Eventually people lose interest and the discussion dies out. Many sources on the internet can be found describing this pattern and offering "netiquette" tips to prevent flame wars (e.g. Shea, no date). There's no question that flaming is a real phenomenon. To some extent, it's surely facilitated by what cues-filtered-out scholars describe. The lack of social presence and accountability in a reduced-cues medium is seen by some as a platform to attack.

However, if flaming were caused by reduced social cues, it ought to be very common online. Yet it is perceived as more common than it actually is. In Rice and Love's (1987) study, only 0.2 percent of the messages were antagonistic. We may overestimate the amount of flaming because single messages may be seen by so many people and because hostile messages are so memorable (Lea et al., 1992). The fact is that most people in online groups are far more likely to be nice than to flame (e.g. Preece & Ghozati, 1998; Rice & Love, 1987). If reduced cues cause flaming, we should also see equal amounts of flaming in all interactions in a medium. But the amount and tolerance of hostility varies tremendously across online groups. Martin Lea and his collaborators (1992) argued that, contrary to the cues filtered out explanation that flaming occurs because of a lack of norms, flaming occurs *because* of norms. Groups with argumentative communication styles encourage people to conform to the group's style, while those with more civil styles invoke more courteous behavior. The predominantly female soap opera discussion group I studied had almost no flaming; what little there was came from outsiders (Baym, 1996, 2000).

Furthermore, rather than occurring in the absence of social norms, people often flame in ways that demonstrate their awareness that they are violating norms (Lea et al., 1992). They may substitute punctuation marks for letters in swear words or use the html inspired "<flame on>" and "</flame off>" designations to bracket the abrasive message. Flames are also used to discipline people for behaving inappropriately, thus maintaining group norms. In some groups, flaming is a form of playful sport. Flaming has been linked to masculinity, or "the chest-thumping display of online egos" (Myers, 1987a: 241), although a content analysis of many messages to Usenet found no gender differences in who flames (Savicki, Lingenfelter, & Kelley, 1996).

Putting social cues into digital communication

Instead of asking what mediation *does to* communication, we can also ask what people *do with* mediated communication. People appropriate media characteristics as resources to pursue social and relational goals (O'Sullivan, 2000). People show feeling and immediacy, have fun, and build and reinforce social structures even in the leanest of text-only media. As a consequence of people's enthusiasm for digital social interaction, developers have created ever-richer means for us to communicate. Even text-only interaction, on which we'll focus here, can be used to accomplish relational and social connection, leaving no question that we can do it with additional cues such as video, images, and voice.

In 1972, just three years into the internet's existence, Carnegie Mellon University professor Scott E. Fahlman proposed that punctuation marks could be combined like this :-) to mark jokes (Anderson, 2005). Fahlman's innovation responded to the now-familiar problem that emotional information can be difficult to convey without facial expression and vocal intonation. Sarcasm can be particularly tricky. Conflict often results. This smiley face, used by many and reviled by some, has spread into elaborate lexicons of *emoticons*, most of which show feelings, but some of which are simply playful. Emoticons have now been built into new media to the extent that when I first typed that punctuation combination, my word processor automatically translated it into this graphical representation: ☺. A glance at any mobile phone's texting service will likewise reveal a wide range of graphic expressions of emotion, almost all of which originated in novel uses of punctuation to illustrate feeling. The people led that innovation in emotional expression. Emoticons have not entirely solved the problem, but they have helped.

There are other ways in which people convey nonverbal social cues when limited to textual communication as well. We use asterisks as brackets, upper-case lettering, and letter and punctuation repetition to indicate emphasis, as in "I am *so* busy" (my word processor automatically transforms the asterisked word into boldface), "I am SO busy," "I am sooooooo busy," or "I am so busy!!!!!!" (e.g. Herring, 2001). People also simply use words or abbreviated phrases to describe their nonverbal reactions in textual media. The people discussing soap operas I studied frequently used phrases like "I laughed so hard everyone knew I wasn't working" or the more oblique "does anyone know how to clean coffee off a keyboard" to describe nonverbal reactions to others' humorous messages. Someone in a music fan group I followed described herself dancing on her couch while listening to the song under discussion. The acronyms LOL (for either "lots of laughs" or "laughing out loud") is even more ubiquitous than its oft-used forerunners ROTFL or the now more common ROFL ("rolling on the floor laughing"). We also display immediacy online, engaging in behaviors that reduce psychological distance and increase affiliation (Mehrabian, 1971).

We show others that we are approachable, and that we are interested in them, through immediacy cues (O'Sullivan et al., 2004). The language of immediacy is informal, filled with non-standard spellings, deletions, casual and slang vocabulary, greetings, and sign offs (Baron, 2008; O'Sullivan et al., 2004), and other linguistic markers. In my own Twitter feed as I write, for instance, highly educated friends have written "yer" (your) and "tho," "Hahaha," "LOL," and "sammich" (sandwich). "Tho" shows how we delete letters. We may also leave out subject pronouns ("gotta go now"), vowels, punctuation, and, in SMS (short message service), spaces, adjectives, and adverbs (Hård af Segerstad, 2005; Ling, 2005). Deletions may be partially driven by the formal limitations of message space and time constraints (especially in synchronous media) and the physical discomforts of too much typing, but they can also create immediacy. Together these many linguistic variations serve as ample resources for building friendly conversationality.

People also appropriate qualities of digital media as resources for play. In her book *Cyberpl@y*, Brenda Danet (2001) traced the playful quality of much online interaction, especially when synchronous, to several influences, including interactivity and synchronicity, anonymity, the lack of clear authorities and formal governing structure, and the legacy of hacker culture with its love of wordplay, puns, irony, flippancy, and irregular uses of typography and spelling. Many people have noted how common humor is in mediated communication contexts, whether it's the use of mobile phones to share dirty jokes amongst teenagers (Oksman & Turtiainen, 2004), the forwarding of humorous emails and links, or displays of creativity in online groups (e.g. Baym, 1995; Myers, 1987a). In a large project (Sudweeks, McLaughlin, & Rafaeli, 1998) in which dozens of researchers from several countries and universities conducted a quantitative content analysis of thousands of messages from international Usenet newsgroups, BITnet lists, and CompuServe, Rafaeli and Sudweeks (1997) found that more than 20 percent of the messages contained humor. In my soap group study, I found that, even in the discussion of a dark storyline the fans disliked and found disturbing, 27 percent of the messages were humorous. Group members indicated in my surveys and in their responses to one another that humor was one of their main criteria for assessing the quality of messages and one another.

There are many other kinds of creative play in textual media as well. In ASCII art, the symbols available on a keyboard are used to draw images. An IRC group Danet (2001) studied used the keyboard in combination with colored fonts to create illustrations with many qualities found in traditional folk designs, such as those in rugs and other textiles. People also invent new words and even dialects in textual interaction. Among the novel words that have entered our lexicon are "spam," "flaming," and "blogging." The widespread lolcat phenomenon, in which short grammatically incorrect phrases rife with misspellings (e.g. "I can haz cheezburger?" or "Literecy cat is amaized at ur perfick grahmar") are juxtaposed with pictures of cats (among other things), has given rise to a new grammatical dialect which can, in fact, be done incorrectly. "You me give cheezburger?" is bad grammar, but it is not lolcat.

As people appropriate the possibilities of textual media to convey social cues, create immediacy, entertain, and show off for one another, they build identities for themselves, build interpersonal relationships, and create social contexts, topics to which we will return in coming chapters. Performing well can bring a person recognition, or at least lead to a sense that there is a real person behind otherwise anonymous text. Our expressions of emotions and immediacy show others that we are real, available, and that we like them, as does our willingness to entertain them. Our playful conventions and in-jokes may create insider symbols that help groups to cohere. These phenomena are only enhanced by the additional cues found in shared video, photography, sound, and other multimedia means of online interaction that have developed over time.

Digital communication as a mixed modality

If comparing mediated communication to face to face communication doesn't work adequately, it might be more fruitful to think of digital communication as a mixed modality that combines elements of communication practices in embodied conversation and in writing. Instead of approaching mediated interaction as face to face communication and finding it wanting, we draw from our existing repertoire of communication skills in other modes to make a medium do what we want it to do as best we can.

Online language has been called an "interactive written register" (Ferrara, Brunner, & Whittemore 1991), a hybrid (Danet, 1997), a creole (Baron, 1998), and an "uncooked linguistic stew" (Baron & Ling, 2003) that blends elements of written and oral language with features that are distinctive to this medium, or at least more common online than in any other language medium. Mediated interaction in several languages (including English, French, Swedish, and Norwegian) resembles both written language and oral conversation (Baron, 2000; Baron & Ling, 2003; Baym, 1996; Danet, 1997; Ferrara et al., 1991; Hård af Segerstad, 2005; Herring, 2001; Ling, 2005).

Online interaction is like writing in many ways. In detailed analyses of naturally occurring messages, Baron (2008) argues that, on balance, emails, instant messages, and text messages look more like writing than speech, but fall on a spectrum in between. Like writing, textual interaction online often bears an address. Messages can be edited prior to transmission. The author and reader are physically (and often temporally) separated. Messages can be read by anonymous readers who may not respond and it is not possible for interlocutors to overlap one another or to interrupt. Context must be created through the prose so that messages are often explicit and complete. There is rarely an assumption of shared physical context. Messages are replicable and can be stored.

On the other hand, there are many ways in which online language resembles speech. As we saw in the discussion of immediacy above, misspellings and deletions often foreground phonetic qualities of language. Despite the challenges to conversational coordination (Herring, 2001), messages are generally related to prior ones, often through turn-taking. The audience is usually able to respond and often does so quickly, resulting in reformulations of original messages. Topics change rapidly. The discourse often feels ephemeral, and often is not stored by recipients despite the capacity for storage.

The specter of a new language form, neither spoken nor written yet both, raises dual fears about the degeneration of spoken conversation and written language. Newspaper articles have worried, for instance, that the brief exchanges of Instant Messaging (IM) will lead to an inability to conduct face to face conversations, or that non-standard spelling and punctuation will decimate grammar as we know it. Teachers in Finland, where text messages are full of non-standard Finnish, worry about negative consequences for student writing (Kasesniemi & Rautiainen, 2002), echoing concerns heard in seemingly every nation that uses these media.

The scant evidence so far does not offer strong reasons for concern. There are far fewer such deviations from standard language forms than people think (Baron & Ling, 2003). Baron (2008) found few abbreviations, acronyms, contractions, misspellings, emoticons, or missing punctuation in American college students' Instant Messages. Furthermore, like flaming, few of the non-standard features of language are due to inattention or lack of awareness of standards (Herring, 2001). Most are deliberate adaptations of the technical and social contexts of interactions for social purposes. The language of mediated interaction is "at most a very minor dialectal variation" (Baron, 2008: 163).

The discourse of fear and language decay surrounding these media (reflected in the rhetorics of new media discussed in the last chapter) can be understood as part of a cultural reaction to the growing informality of public life. Baron (2008) argues that, culturally, formality has increasingly been replaced by casualness, something that extends to writing across media. Writing standards, she argues, are declining as we rarely linger over the written word. Social attitudes to proofreading and perfect writing have changed so that writing is done more quickly. "Computers are not the cause of contemporary language attitudes and practices," Baron writes (2008: 171), but, "like signal boosters, they magnify ongoing trends."

People also usually understand that not all textual digital media, or circumstances in which they are used, are alike, and adapt accordingly. Messages in IM, chat, and SMS are considerably shorter than those in most other forms of online interaction, for instance, due to the temporal and software structures of those modalities. Any instance of digital language use depends on the technology, the purpose of the interaction, the norms of the group, the communication style of the speakers' social groups offline, and the idiosyncrasies of individuals. There is no standardized "digital language."

However, even if there is little reason for concern about whole-sale devolutions of language in other contexts, there is still disagreement about which elements of online style are appropri-ate to use when. These are value questions we are still resolving. In one particularly prominent example, Jerry Yang, the CEO of Yahoo!, wrote an entirely lower-case email to all employees to announce the layoff of thousands of workers. Yang's letter spread widely across the internet where the lack of capitalization generated controversy. While some saw it as a means of creating immediacy, thus showing compassion for the workers, and others saw it as a goofy personality quirk, some found all-lower-case entirely inap-propriate in these professional and difficult circumstances. The gossip site Valleywag (Thomas, 2009), for instance, offered the headline "Jerry Yang's incompetent layoff memo" and decried the use of "all lowercase letters, as is Yang's too-lazy-for-the-shift-key wont."

When we broaden this discussion to include the many means of non-textual communication that have developed since most of these studies were published, we can see that what was once a complex hybrid between writing and speech has become even more complicated than I've presented here. Increasingly, our online language involves "remediation" (e.g. Fornås et al., 2002), in which we blend and incorporate styles from conversations and writing with stylistic and formal elements of film, television, music videos, and photography, and other genres and practices.

Contextual influences on online communication

Thus far we've focused on technological and social drivers of online communication. Communication is also shaped by larger social forces we have incorporated into our own identities and carry with us into our mediated interactions. A quick look at how gender and culture play out online speaks to how social contexts shape and are shaped by mediated communication.

Gender

All cultures have different customs, rules, and expectations for behavior from men and women. Early discourses of the internet suggested that gender might cease to be meaningful in a cyberme-diated world, or that it might be entirely reinvented. Some online contexts do take gender as a subject for linguistic play. One much-studied Multi-User Domain, Lambda MOO, offers participants multiple gender options for their identity, each with its own set of pronouns (Danet, 1998). In addition to male, female, and neuter, people can choose to identify as: either, Spivak, splat, plural, ego-tistical, royal, or 2nd person. Third person descriptions of each of these options would be he, she, it, s/he, E, e*, they, I, we, and you.

Several language-oriented researchers have compared men's and women's mediated messages and concluded that gender influences mediated interaction just as it influences unmediated communi-cation. Rather than being liberated from gender, people perform gender through the ways they communicate (e.g. Herring, 1996). Most studies of gendered communication find men and women are far more similar in their communication than different, but women are socialized to attend more to relational dimensions of conversation while men are reared to specialize in the informative dimensions (Burleson & Kunkel, 2006; Kunkel & Burleson, 1999).

Not surprisingly, gender differences appear in mediated interaction. Statistical analysis of large samples of communication from Usenet groups found that the influence of gender on language style was present, but modest (Savicki et al., 1996). Kasesniemi and Rautiainen (2002: 185) described Finnish girls' text messages as "full of social softening, extra words and emotional sharing of experiences. Boys tend to write only about what has happened, and where and how ... girls contemplate the reasons." Finnish women are more likely than men to keep mobile phones on at night (Puro, 2002), suggesting they see them as relational tools while men tie them to information that ends with the workday. Women are more likely to use a supportive/attenuated style oriented towards affiliation. Messages written by women are more likely to include qualifications, justifications, apologies, and expressions of support (Herring, 1996). Women's IM closings take twice as many turns and are nearly three times as long as male closings. Women are also nearly three times more likely to begin SMS interactions with openings (Baron, 2008; Baron & Ling, 2003). In her work comparing discussion groups oriented towards male and female topics, Larson (2003) found that women used a wider range of nonverbal cues online than men. Groups with more men use more factually oriented language and calls for action, less self-disclosure, and fewer attempts at tension prevention and reduction (Savicki et al., 1996). Men may be more likely to use an adversarial style in their messages (Herring, 2001), though the data on flaming is mixed (Savicki et al., 1996). One MUD developed a term for the behavior of its male members: "MAS" for "Male Answer Syndrome" (Kendall, 2002). Gender can also influence how messages are perceived: men may be more likely to see aggressive messages as evidence of freedom of speech, candor, and healthy debate, while women are more likely to see them as hostile and unconstructive (Herring, 1996).

Gender differences persist online. So too does sexism. Women with unpopular positions are routinely attacked for being women while men with unpopular ideas are attacked for their ideas (Gurak, 1997). Women are depicted as sexual objects. When someone mentions seeing a woman in one MUD, for instance, a typical response is "did you spike 'er?" (Kendall, 2002: 85). When people sell their characters in role-playing games, female avatars go for 10 percent less than their male counterparts, even when they have comparable skill levels (Castronova, 2004).

Culture

Gender has received a good deal of attention from scholars interested in new technology. The topic of cultural identity, including nationality, language, and race and ethnicity, has not. Miller and Slater's (2000) ethnographic analysis is an exception, showing how Trinidadian identity permeated online interaction. "Trinis" living both at home and abroad communicated in a style that displayed "being Trini and representing Trinidad" for one another and for outsiders. This ranged from engaging in "limin'," an often risqué form of playful banter, to including links to Trinidadian national sites on their personal webpages. Ananda Mitra's (1997) analysis of the soc.culture.indian Usenet group showed how diasporic Indians used communication that both maintained their Indian identity and recreated India's internal ethnic divides.

Lisa Nakamura (2002) and David Silver (2000) have drawn attention to how race is represented or erased through the interfaces of online spaces. Race is often "routed around" online, rather than brought to the front (Silver, 2000). For example, many online sites that make users select gender and even species do not make them select race. This may be celebrated as an erasure of an unnecessary social division, but it can also be read as an assumption that most users are White. Listings of discussion groups on Yahoo! Groups are typical in that they designate many racial and ethnic groups, constructing for their users a range of social identities with which they may or may not identify. "White" does not appear in Yahoo!'s list of racial and ethnic categories. Discussion groups that do label themselves "White" are often supremacist. Like sexism, racism thrives online, and groups that do self-identify as "White" are often replete with horrifying demonstrations of racial animosity towards others. Even when one can select a non-White race, online spaces often offer highly stereotypical portrayals

(Nakamura, 2002). Asian men, for instance, are frequently sword wielding or nerdy. Asian women, so often the subjects of online pornography, often appear as passive sex toys.

Cultural identity also manifests through the language we use. As discussed in chapter 1, the internet was created in the English-speaking world, and the influence and spread of English online remains disproportionate to its speakers. It's only in the last few years that English has come to represent less than half of the internet's language, but it is still (for now) the most common language used online. Until recently, online writing was restricted to the ASCII character set, which is designed exclusively for the Latin alphabet. With the advent of Unicode, people can now write with other alphabets; however, this technology is neither available to nor used by all. The result has sometimes been considered a form of "typographical imperialism" (Herring & Danet, 2003) with potential social, political, economic, and linguistic consequences. For instance, I've mentioned the outcry about the devolution of language in Greece and its echoes of Socrates' warnings about the alphabet. This centers on "Greeklish," the online version of written Greek using the Latin alphabet, which has been decried in Greek papers for destroying the language (Koutsogiannis & Mitsikopoulou, 2003).

The business Translate to Success (2009) compiled data from a variety of surveys of internet users to estimate that, in 2004, 38.3 percent of internet users spoke English. Chinese, Japanese, and Korean are also popular, constituting 11.2 percent, 10 percent, and 4.1 percent respectively. Only 1 percent of the world's internet users speak Arabic. Fewer than 0.1 percent speak any African language. An effort to conduct a language census of blogs (www.hirank.com/semantic-indexing-project/census/lang.html, accessed October 1, 2009; *Languages*, n.d.) indexed over 2 million blogs. More than half of these were in English, followed in dramatically smaller numbers by those in Catalan, French, Spanish, and Portuguese. German, Italian, Chinese, Farsi, Japanese, and Dutch were the only other languages found in more than 10,000 blogs each. Herring, Paolillo, Ramos-Vielba et al. (2007) studied blogs on the site LiveJournal, where two-thirds of users report being outside the

USA and pages can be set to appear in 32 different languages. They found that the blogs were 84 percent English, 11 percent Russian, 0.4 percent Portuguese, 0.3 percent Finnish, Spanish, Dutch, and Japanese, and 2.3 percent mixed language. All other languages combined only made up 0.8 percent of the site's user-generated content.

These statistics are obviously profoundly skewed in comparison to the distribution of speakers in the global population, and reflect economic and social conditions in these parts of the world. The overrepresentation of languages used in wealthy countries, especially English, has often given rise to a sentiment that the internet represents a further colonization of poor nations by those with greater wealth, particularly the United States. Many of the world's voices and communicative styles are simply absent from mediated communication.

Summary

Messages in textual media we shaped by both technological and social qualities, both of which affect the consequences it may have. From a deterministic perspective, the two primary forces that influence online language use are the paucity of social cues, or media leanness, and the potential asynchronicity of a medium. Together, these are taken to have a host of effects, foremost among them decreasing the intimacy or personal quality of interactions (and subsequently relationships) and increasing the hostility of mediated interactions. There is a grain of truth in those claims, but they are inadequate to explain what people do with language online. Rather than giving up and accepting limited cues as a directive to live without emotion and caring in their mediated interactions, a communication imperative inspires people to appropriate the cues that are on offer in creative ways so they can show feeling, play, perform, and create identities, relationships, and group contexts.

Social forces, both online and off, shape language use online and in mobile texting, their signal boosted by mediation. People's familiarity with the medium is an influence, as are their motivations for participating. Relational and group contexts, which may themselves be shaped through online discourse, matter. Most online communication happens against a backdrop of a shared history, whether that involves two individuals or a group that has had time to develop norms to guide appropriate behavior. People draw on long-standing language practices in other media like writing and oral conversation to guide their verbal and nonverbal activity in new media. Social identities including (but by no means limited to) gender and culture affect how people act and how their messages are perceived. The ways people communicate in these media have in turn shaped the media themselves, as developers have responded to user creativity by automating emoticons, adding new ways to represent social cues (e.g. color, images, sound), and making it possible to use non-Roman alphabets through the technologies.

In sum, mediated communication demonstrates many new qualities, but continues to display and reinforce the broader cultural forces that influence messages in all contexts. As we will explore in the next chapter, reduced cues may on occasion allow individuals to pass as something or someone they are not, but the social structures that shape us and our potentials manifest in our communication, identities, relationships, communities, and networks online just as they do offline.

4

Communities and networks

After inventing one-to-one communication systems, it took the developers of what became the internet almost no time to develop platforms for group communication. Among the first such groups was SF-Lovers, a mailing list for science fiction fans. Accompanied by influential bulletin board systems such as the Bay Area counter-culture hangout, The Well (Rheingold, 1993), and early multiplayer games, these group communication platforms were followed by thousands, then millions, of topically organized mailing lists, Usenet newsgroups, and websites. The advent of social network sites (SNSs) in the late 1990s provided another platform for groups and simultaneously posed challenges for online groups by foregrounding more loosely bound networks of individuals.

Many online groups develop a strong sense of group member-ship. They serve as bases for the creation of new relationships as people from multiple locations gather synchronously or asynchro-nously to discuss topics of shared interest, role play, or just hang out. Participants have extolled the benefits of being able to form new connections with others regardless of location and to easily find others with common interests, the round-the-clock avail-ability of these groups, and the support they provide. Members of these groups often describe them as "communities." Internet proponents such as Howard Rheingold (1993) touted a new age of "virtual community" in which webs of personal connection transcended time and distance to create meaningful new social formations. My own research on the newsgroup rec.arts.tv.soaps (r.a.t.s.) conceptualized the group as a community.

Given its emotional force, it's not surprising that this use of "community" generated strong counter-reactions from those such

as Lockard (1997: 225) who warned that "to accept only communication in place of a community's manifold functions is to sell
our common faith in community vastly short." Early critics such
as Stoll (1995) raised fears of a "silicon snake oil" that replaced
genuine and deep connections with shallow and inadequate substitutes. The specter of people isolated indoors substituting Gergen's
"floating world" of connection for meaningful contact with their
neighbors sends a shudder through those concerned that, as
Robert Putnam (1995) famously put it, we are already doing far too
much "bowling alone."

If you hear echoes of the hopes and concerns about mediated
interaction that have reverberated through the history of communication technologies, you should. As we've seen in previous
chapters, people tend to doubt the authenticity of social connections sustained through new media and question their impact on
interpersonal, local, and national civic and political engagement.
Historical changes occurring in conjunction with and facilitated by
communication technologies have led many to worry that people
are losing meaningful connections to their local communities,
with towns, cities, and nations suffering the consequences. Digital
technologies hold the potential to engage us more closely in meaningful communal connections but, inasmuch as they might take
us away from embodied local interactions, they could threaten to
damage the real thing.

In this chapter we'll look at how people organize into groups and
networks online. First, we'll ask what is meant when people say
"community," and what it means to apply that term to an online
group. We turn then to social networks, exploring how these more
recent platforms have afforded more personalized and diffuse
yet centralized connections. In closing the chapter we'll look at
how the use of digital media seems to affect participation in local
communities.

Online community

What did it mean when YouTube, with its millions of users, promi-
nently featured the term "community" on its navigation bar, as

though all of its users were united into a common group through mere use of the site? What kind of "community" was being invoked when the digital services company Sparta Networks (n.d.) boasted on their website that they built a client "a highly scalable, function-rich, flexible online community . . . in less than a third of the time it would have taken them to build the community internally?" These technological definitions of "community" appeal to developers and also to marketers (Preece & Maloney-Krichmar, 2003) who can create a site, call it a "community," and hope to reap the benefits of the term's warm connotations without having to deal with questions of what actually happens on-site. Different technological platforms do lend themselves to different sorts of group formations, and differences in digital affordances lead to differences in group behavior. Yet one need only peek below the surface of any one online platform to see that technologically based definitions of "community" fall apart in the face of variety. YouTube, as Burgess and Green (2009) show, is far from a single collective. Instead it is comprised of many subgroups, each with their own practices and purposes, which are sometimes at odds with the other groups. Thus, when Oprah decided to join YouTube, many of the amateur media producers resented her and her fans' presence, just as the female vloggers resented the sexist commenting practices of male subgroups with which they had to contend. The mere existence of an interactive online forum is not community, and those who participate using one platform may comprise very different groups.

Whether you are willing to consider any digitally based group a "community" depends first and foremost on which of many definitions of "community" you choose. Articles and books on digital community often begin by noting that no one has ever been able to agree what exactly "community" means. "Ever since sociological theorist Ferdinand Tönnies declared community to be an essential condition for the development of close, primary social bonds," wrote Mary Chayko (2008: 6), "sociologists have not been able to agree on how, or whether, definitions of community should be updated." Despite the term's openness to a variety of interpretations, it remains useful. Chayko conducted electronic interviews with 87 people who self-identified as active users of group communication online, in order to explore their perspectives of mediated social dynamics. Although she did not use the word "community" in her interview questions (2008: 212–13), her interviewees repeatedly invoked it to describe their online experiences, saying things like "I feel I am part of a tight-knit community" and "You can definitely feel the community on the board" (2008: 7). Like Chayko, I am reluctant to drop the term altogether. "Community" has provided a resonant handle for developers, analysts, marketers, and even critics as they've tried to understand online groups. Rather than debate which definition is correct, and hence whether or not online communities are "real," I will identify five qualities found in both online groups and many definitions of community that make the term resonate for online contexts. These include the sense of space, shared practice, shared resources and support, shared identities, and interpersonal relationships.

Space

Those who argue online groups cannot be communities often consider common geography a necessary condition of "community." From early on, geographical communities such as Berkeley and Santa Monica, California, turned to the internet as a means of building local community, creating community networks to foster civic engagement and provide access for those without internet connections. Schuler (1996) runs through several examples of efforts to create online networks to support local communities. One of the earliest, Santa Monica's PEN system had five objectives, including providing city residents with: easy electronic access to public information; an alternative means of communication, delivery and creating awareness of public services; and the opportunity to learn about computer technology. The PEN system also sought "to provide an electronic forum for participation in discussions of issues and concerns of residents in order to promote an enhanced sense of community" (quoted in Schuler, 1996: 120).

Most online groups are not so tied to geographical space, yet people who are involved in online groups often think of them as shared places. The feeling that online groups meeting on software and hardware platforms constitute "spaces" is integral to the language often used to describe the internet. Consider the term "cyberspace," coined by science fiction author William Gibson, or the western United States metaphor in the subtitle of Rheingold's now classic 1993 book *The Virtual Community: Homesteading on the Electronic Frontier*.

The metaphor of space is particularly applicable in visual online environments such as massively multiplayer online role playing games (MMORPGs) where fictional worlds built through code are experienced as semi-physical realities. Second Life, where users create buildings, parks, and other emulations of physical spaces, also lends itself to spatial understandings of "community." Schuler (1996) organizes the second chapter of his book around Ray Oldenburg's concept of a "third place." Similarly, in their analysis of two MMORPGs, Steinkuehler and Williams (2006) use Oldenburg's ideas to argue that these environments function similarly to the "cafes, coffee shops, community centers, beauty parlors, general stores, bars and hangouts that get you through the day" in well-functioning cities and towns (Oldenburg, 1989: front cover). Third places, neither work nor home, are vital sites of informal social life, critical to social cohesion. Steinkuehler and Williams's analysis of MMORPGs as third places shows how they provide sites of neutral ground, equal status, sociable conversation, easy access, known regulars, playful interaction, (sometimes) homely aesthetics, and a homelike atmosphere.

Textual groups can also be metaphorically based on space, as was the case in the official board for fans of television show *Buffy the Vampire Slayer* documented by Stephanie Tuszynski in her ethnographic film *IRL: In Real Life*. This board was called "The Bronze" after a hangout in the television show. Members Tuszynski interviewed frequently referred to the board as a place, one even laughing at herself for saying goodbye to her partner before walking down the hall to go to the Bronze, as though she were leaving the apartment to go elsewhere. Furthermore, online groups can be organized with reference to geographical location. People form groups to discuss national and regional issues (e.g. Mitra's 1997 analysis of soc.culture.indian or Gajjala's 2004 work on SAWNet, a discussion forum for women from East Asia). People also form groups to discuss cultural materials tied to particular regions, as I've described in the context of Swedish independent music's international fans (Baym, 2007).

Practice

A metaphorical sense of shared space is thus one criterion that people use when they label digitally mediated groups "communities." Community can also be found in the habitual and usually unconscious practices – routinized behaviors – that group members share. Communities of practice include occupational, educational, and recreational groups as well as regional ones (e.g. Dundes, 1977; Lave & Wenger, 1991). Because language is the primary tool through which digitally mediated groups cohere, the concept of "speech community," which foregrounds shared communication practices, has been particularly useful for many of us studying online groups. Speech communities have distinctive patterns of language use which enact and recreate a cultural ideology that underpins them (Philipsen, 1992).

Online speech communities share ways of speaking that capture the meanings that are important to them and the logics that underlie their common sensibilities. Groups share insider lingo including acronyms, vocabulary words, genres, styles, and forms of play. Lynn Cherny (1999) conducted an extensive ethnography of a MOO she called ElseMOO, paying particular attention to how the language use embodied and evoked the community within the site. In my book *Tune In, Log On* (Baym, 2000), I wrote about a soap opera fan group (r.a.t.s.) on Usenet. Like Cherny, I spent years reading the group and conducted close analysis of the ways in which language created a social context akin to community. Members of r.a.t.s. used many terms comprehensible to insiders, including the acronym "IOAS" for "It's Only A Soap" and numerous nicknames for characters. Members of The Bronze, like members of so many online groups, developed communication genres such as the morning "shout out" listing all new members of the group and the "question of the day" posed by the same individual each morning. Though, like YouTube, I would not consider Twitter a single community, its users do share some practices, shaped both by technological affordances (the 140-character limit) and by other internet trends such as lolcat (see chapter 3). The power of being able to speak like a Twitter insider was evident when the four founders of Swedish file-sharing site The Pirate Bay went on trial in 2009. One defendant twittered from the courtroom. With posts such as "EPIC WINNING LOL" he quickly won the hearts of his Twitter followers (if not the court), who saw one of their own in his use of language. They did not win the trial, but the Swedish election of a member of the Pirate Party to the European Parliament in the wake of their conviction was evidence of the popular support they had gained.

These terms and genres are markers of insider status and hence help to forge group identity (see further discussion of this below). They also indicate groups' core values. IOAS did not just mean "it's only a soap opera," it also meant that the group valued soap operas and understood that one could be involved enough to find them frustrating yet not be the lifeless idiots represented by the soap viewer stereotype. The term simultaneously validated group members' shared love of the genre, self-representation as intelligent, and their shared frustrations. The Bronze shout out demonstrated their openness to new members. Twitterers use of "epic" demonstrates the shared values of humor and irreverence.

Shared practices entail *norms* for the appropriate use of communication. Ongoing groups develop standards that guide members' behavior. Violations of these norms are often met with critical response from other users. In an early study, McLauglin, Osborne, and Smith (1995) collected messages from Usenet in which participants had been castigated for misbehavior. Analyzing those instances, they identified several issues that spanned Usenet groups, including incorrect use of technology, bandwidth waste, network-wide conventions, newsgroup-specific conventions, ethical violations, inappropriate language, and factual errors. Online groups that discuss television shows and movies often have a norm that the word "spoilers" should be included in the subject lines of posts which give away the story ahead of time. This enables those who don't want the show spoiled by this advance information to avoid such posts. Other groups are devoted entirely to sharing spoilers.

In the last chapter, we saw groups differ in their attitude towards flaming (Lea et al., 1992); the soap opera group I studied would have none of it, while other groups tolerate and even encourage it. The discussion board for my favorite band tolerates a great deal of rudeness, particularly when people violate norms, but attends carefully to an implicit norm that people must be thanked when they share materials with the group. Users of r.a.t.s. shared a commitment to friendliness, which could be seen in the details of how they disagreed with one another. Their disagreements were packed with qualification ("I might be wrong but I thought that . . ."), partial agreement ("I agree that . . ., but I still thought that . . ."), and other linguistic strategies designed to minimize offense and maximize affiliation (Baym, 1996). Group members do not have to think about these norms as they formulate their messages. Instead, becoming a group insider involves a process of being socialized to these norms and values so that they guide one's communication without having to be considered.

Social norms also emerge in social network sites (SNSs). Fono and Raynes-Goldie (2006) interviewed users of LiveJournal about their reasons for friending people on that site and the issues that arise around friending. boyd (2006) interviewed users of MySpace and Friendster. Both studies found friending norms, although they were not uniform and, as we will return to in chapter 6, caused confusion and interpersonal conflict. Donath (2007) argues that SNSs develop norms for what constitutes truth in terms of "the mores of our community." Humphreys (2007) observed the short-lived location-sensitive SNS Dodgeball for one year and performed in-depth interviews with users in seven American cities. She found that there were norms regulating things such as how often one should post one's location to the network. Just as the norms around friending are uncertain, "normative Dodgeball use is not only emerging but contested"; subgroups "may have different tolerance levels, expectations, and definitions of acceptable or 'correct' Dodgeball use" (Humphreys, 2007).

Community norms of practice are displayed, reinforced, negotiated, and taught through members' shared behaviors. They are also enshrined through FAQs (Frequently Asked Questions files). Early on, these appeared as regularly occurring posts in message boards. Web boards often include them as a link. Hansen and his collaborators studied a question-and-answer mailing list for web developers that also maintained a wiki repository that worked as a FAQ and as an alternative space that allowed members to keep the list discussion on-topic (Hansen, Ackerman, Resnick, & Munson, 2007). They performed both qualitative thematic analysis and quantitative content analysis of all the wiki pages as well as samples from several thousand of the group's 90,000 emails, and conducted semi-structured interviews. They found that the wikis served several normative functions in the group. When people broached irresolvable disputes over topics such as font size, they could be gently referred to the wiki. This allowed the list to avoid irresolvable "holy wars," maintain the "friendly and professional tone," and socialize new members without losing old members who had been through those questions many times before.

Online groups also share norms for what constitutes skilled communicative practice. The Pirate Bay founder who knew to use the phrase "epic winning" and the acronym "LOL" demonstrated not just his insider status, but also his skill as a twitterer. Participants in r.a.t.s valued humor and insight in their posts, and, in surveys I conducted, particularly funny posters were those most frequently mentioned as "good" contributors. In fan communities, those who write particularly good fan fiction might be celebrated, while those who give especially helpful advice might be considered the best contributors to support communities. Friends who post status updates at the right frequency with the right mix of humor, self-deprecation, and thoughtfulness might be most appreciated on Facebook.

Normative standards always implicate power structures. Hierarchies form online, giving some people more say than others in creating and regulating behavioral standards within group contexts. Stivale, for example, examined the variants of what counts as spam in LambdaMOO and argued that "the ambiguity of what is appropriate or not suggests once again the ongoing struggle between centripetal and centrifugal forces, i.e. forces that seek some unified central 'command' versus those seeking to contest such unification from the margins" (Stivale, 1997: 139). Many groups are moderated, meaning that power structures are both explicit and built into the group's very structure. Some of the norm-maintaining jobs that moderators do include keeping the group on-topic, deleting posts that they deem inappropriate or distracting, and fixing problematic formatting. In unmoderated groups, power structures may be implicit and emergent (Preece & Maloney-Krichmar, 2003). The contrast between this and optimistic predictions that the absence of social cues in online interaction would eliminate hierarchy and render all participants equal should be obvious.

Social norms are also rooted within the behavioral contexts in which users live, as we saw in the last chapter's discussion of how social identities influence online communication. On social network sites (SNSs), where people may be "aware that their friends and colleagues are looking at their self-presentation," they are likely to feel pressured to conform to those groups' norms (Donath, 2007). Walther, Van Der Heide, Kim and Westerman (2008) conducted an experiment in which they first had focus groups describe what constituted good and bad peer behaviors. They then manipulated Facebook profiles to demonstrate those behaviors and assessed perceptions of those profiles. They found that people did rely on societal and peer group standards when forming impressions online. Wall posts describing excessive and questionable behavior result in more negative perceptions, although this was only true for women (at least amongst the college-aged Americans in the study). In an analysis of the metadata from 362 million fully anonymized private messages and "pokes" exchanged by 4.2 million North American Facebook users through that site, Golder, Wilkinson, and Huberman (2007) found that messaging was guided by strong temporal rhythms that were often grounded in local norms. For instance, messaging took place at night and peaked Tuesdays and Wednesdays and was at its lowest during the "college student weekend" beginning mid-afternoon Friday and lasting through mid-afternoon Sunday.

Shared resources and support

Communities were often defined as "composed of broadly based relationships in which each community member felt securely able to obtain a wide variety of help" (Wellman, 1988: 97). The supportive exchange of resources is often implied when people use the term "community" in digital contexts. Closely related to social support is "social capital" (Coleman, 1988). Social capital, as Ellison, Steinfeld, and Lampe (2007) explain, is "an elastic term with a variety of definitions." In essence, it refers to the resources people attain because of their network of relationships. When people provide and receive social support in online groups, they are contributing to one another's accumulated social capital. Social capital may be either "bonding" or "bridging" (Putnam, 1995). Bridging capital is exchanged between people who differ from one another and do not share strong relationships. The internet lends itself to and expands the potential for this kind of capital. In contrast, bonding capital is usually exchanged between people in close relationships. While the former is a "sociological lubricant," the latter is "a kind of social superglue" (Steinkuehler & Williams, 2006). Many online groups provide bridging capital, exchanged in relationships that are highly specialized, yet it is also common to find members of online communities and social networks providing one another with the sort of emotional support often found in close relationships.

Social support offers many benefits to its recipients. Documented positive effects include better psychological adjustment, higher perceptions of self-efficacy, better coping, improved task performance, better disease resistance and recovery, and lowered risk of mortality (Burleson & MacGeorge, 2002). Some online communities are explicitly support groups. Forums abound for people with medical conditions, addiction, traumas, and other debilitating or stigmatizing life circumstances. Walther and Boyd (2002) conducted an email survey of a sampling of people who had posted to Usenet support groups. Their research identifies four motivations for people to seek this kind of support online, including the security provided by anonymity, the ease of access to these groups, the ability to manage one's interaction within them, and the social distance from others. Online support can thus allow people access to bonding and bridging resources without the entanglements and threats of close relationships. These groups are also important for those without local support groups.

The provision of social support is common even in groups that are not explicitly designated as supportive (Wellman & Gulia, 1999). There are several, often overlapping, kinds of social support (Cutrona & Russell, 1990). *Social integration* or *network* support:

> enables people to feel part of a group whose members have common interests and concerns. Such relationships reflect more casual friendships, which enable a person to engage in various forms of social and recreational activities. (Cutrona & Russell, 1990: 322)

Online fans and hobbyist groups exemplify this, as their very existence is predicated on a desire to organize around common interests for social and recreational purposes. Consider the *Survivor* spoiler fan "knowledge community" described by Jenkins (2006). Members of this group collaborated to figure out the identities of all the contestants and even the winner of the sixth season's contest before the entrants had been officially announced or the first show had aired. In the short term, this group was "just having fun on a Friday night participating in an elaborate scavenger hunt involving thousands of participants who all interact in a global village." In the long term, Jenkins posits that they were coming to understand "how they may deploy the new kinds of power that are emerging from participation within knowledge communities" (2006: 29). The recreational information exchanged amongst fans online becomes a form of subcultural capital that can bolster individuals' status within and outside of the fan group (Kibby, 2010).

Emotional support represents "the ability to turn to others for comfort and security during times of stress, leading the person to feel that he or she is cared for by others" (Cutrona & Russell, 1990: 322). In one striking example, Heather Spohr, a prominent "mommy blogger," had been writing about her daughter since her premature birth at 29 weeks. She and her readers built strong connections. When Spohr's daughter passed away unexpectedly at

17 months, the *Los Angeles Times* (Bermudez, 2009) described an outpouring of support that crashed the servers and generated more than $20,000 in donations to the March of Dimes, a nonprofit organization working to help prevent birth defects. While emotional support may be more common in explicit support groups, a content analysis of diverse online groups found that most demonstrate empathic communication and provide emotional support (Preece & Ghozati, 1998).

Esteem support bolsters "a person's sense of competence or self-esteem" through the provision of "individual positive feedback on his or her skills and abilities or expressing a belief that the person is capable" (Cutrona & Russell, 1990: 322). McKenna and Bargh (1998) surveyed people who posted to Usenet groups for homosexuals. They found that newsgroups contributed to "identity demarginalization." As people participated within the newsgroups and received positive feedback for their gay identities, their self-acceptance increased and sense of estrangement dropped. As a direct result, they were more likely to come out to their loved ones. McKenna and Bargh concluded that the anonymity of online groups allows people to engage in riskier self-disclosure and, when that is affirmed, such groups can create positive changes in people's self-concepts.

Informational support offers "advice or guidance concerning possible solutions to a problem" (Cutrona & Russell, 1990: 322). Advice may be about topics as diverse as writing CSS or managing one's love life. Much of the communication on Oprah's web board exemplifies informational (and emotional) support, as seen in this exchange when Brokenhearted girl wrote about her ex-boyfriend's on-again off-again affections for her. Phyllis g advised:

> Listen to what all frosting1112 had to say to you today . . . she is wise and what she said is right-on!! I, too, think your ex-boyfriend is trying to keep you hanging on!! Guys do this all the time. They will break your heart . . . knowing that you love them. and then feel some sort of . . . male "thing" when you cry about them.. It makes me sick!! Girl.. Maybe it's time you just start setting some of those boundaries for yourself!! Your pain is very genuine to me. I know and can feel threw the computer and threw your words that you need help . . . but . . . if you keep focusing on him and never

really try working this out for yourself. You are going to continue to stay sick!! And, you are sick . . . he is like a drug for you. YOU got to make a step . . . toward recovery!! He is an addiction!! (*Phyllis g*)

Frosting 1112 later returned to the thread, offering emotional support:

Hi again. Hope things are getting better for you girl.. You still sound a little confused and upset to me.. I hope and shall keep you in my prayers. And know God will bring you peace if you let him!! (*Frosting 1112*)

In response, Brokenhearted girl provided the others in the thread with esteem support:

I wanted to thank you all for you beautiful reply. I could only hope to be as beautiful as the sweet spirit that I know from all of you!!

This exchange demonstrates the cyclical and self-reinforcing nature of much supportive behavior in online communities, a point I'll return to in discussing people's motivations for providing strangers and casual acquaintances with resources.

When people support one another with money, by doing things for them, and by providing them lodging and other services, Cutrona and Russell call this *tangible aid*. Though this is less common in online groups than the other forms of support, it occurs regularly and frequently. For instance, when one of the regular writers at Daily Kos, a left-leaning political blogging site, suffered extreme damages to his home, members of the site sent him money to help him to recover. People often provide traveling members of online groups places to stay or at least meals, when they visit their towns.

As they share resources in public group contexts, people participating in online groups collaboratively build a replenishing repository of public goods that can be used by unknown recipients one might never encounter again and whom one can't expect to reciprocate immediately (Kollock, 1999). One might ask why people do this. It makes obvious sense to take the time and financial and emotional risks to support those you already know and love, but why provide this kind of support to people you hardly know or may not know at all? One reason may be what Cutrona and Russell

(1990: 332) refer to as a sixth form of social support: supporting others gives people the *feeling that they are needed*. Helping others online may give people a sense of efficacy (Kollock, 1999). Offering support to others now may lead to receiving support should you ever go looking for it in the future (Kollock, 1999). Being a skilled provider of resources can also increase people's status and prestige within online groups (Matzat, 2004). On the board for my favorite band, one member gained high standing because he regularly searched the internet for relevant videos and photographs and then shared them with the others, solving the ongoing informational problem fans face of never being able to know enough about that which they love.

Shared identities

The sense of shared space, rituals of shared practices, and exchange of social support all contribute to a feeling of community in digital environments. Shared identities are also important. These include personalities and roles assumed by individuals. Identities also include a shared sense of who "we" are that may be pre-existing or develop within a group. Many regulars take on specific roles. Some of the most common roles are "local experts, answer people, conversationalists, fans, discussion artists, flame warriors, and trolls" (Welser, Gleave, Fischer, & Smith, 2007). People assume roles by enacting consistent and systematic behaviors that serve a particular function. I've mentioned the fan in a music group who regularly hunted down and shared videos and photographs of the band. In r.a.t.s., one woman took on the role of welcome-wagon, greeting all new contributors with an enthusiastic response designed to encourage them to continue participating, a role seen also in The Bronze, where one contributor posted the "shout out" to new posters each morning. The forums on Last.fm were filled with people playing the role of "Last.fm fan," systematically defending the site's staff and developers against criticism while telling the critics that the site was free and, if they didn't like it, they should leave. In the community of fans of Swedish music, a particularly powerful and recognizable identity is that of mp3 blogger, and the few who claim this role gain status amongst the fans, as well as with the musicians, labels, and others professionally involved with Swedish independent music (Baym, 2007; Baym & Burnett, 2009).

Welser and his colleagues (2007) were interested in whether they could identify people who play roles within Usenet communities from structural information alone. Based on a sample of almost 6,000 messages from three different newsgroups, they determined that several roles could be identified from metadata. "Answer people" frequently responded yet never initiated, while "discussion people" both initiated and responded. Furthermore, there was very little communication amongst the individuals in the threads to which "answer people" contributed, while there was a great deal amongst participants in "discussion people's" threads. They conclude that roles have "behavioral and structural 'signatures'" (Welser et al., 2007). From the point of view of regular participants, these structural signatures are less visible than the fact that the answer person is a regular, one who can be counted on to provide informational support when a new participant asks for it.

The most common role in most, if not all, online communities is that of "lurker," the person who reads but never posts. The Scandinavian music newszine that serves as a hub of sorts for that fan community, It's a Trap!, had a message board. Of the 30,000 people who looked at that board each month, fewer than 100 ever left comments or contributed. Most who do post to an online group do so rarely. In r.a.t.s., more than half who posted did so only once, while the top 10 percent of posters wrote half of all messages (Baym, 2000). Hansen et al. (2007) found that the top 4 percent of the CSS-L mailing list wrote half of the messages.

Given the prevalence of this silent majority, Preece, Nonnecke, and Andrews (2004) investigated the reasons for lurkers' silence. Their survey of a sample from 375 online groups found no differences between lurkers and posters in terms of age, gender, education, or employment. They did find, though, that lurkers were less likely to read the group because they sought answers and less likely to feel they attained the benefits from group membership that they expected, felt a lower sense of group belonging, and respected the other participants less than did the posters. Ironically, posters were more likely to consider lurkers part of the community than were lurkers themselves. The vast majority of lurkers had not intended to read without posting from the outset (only 13.2 percent did). Their silence was motivated by a variety of reasons which Preece et al. (2004) collapse into five. First, many lurkers felt they were already getting what they needed from the group without contributing their own messages. Some felt they needed to get to know the group better. For instance, they may not have felt they knew enough about the group's norms or the topic of discussion, or may have felt shy. Several indicated that they believed they were contributing to the well-being of the community by staying silent when they had nothing to offer. Technical problems with posting were a fourth reason for lurking. Some simply couldn't make the software work or did not know how to post their own messages. Finally, people indicated that they lurked because they did not like the group's dynamics, perhaps because the participants seemed different from themselves, or because they feared aggressive responses.

Groups sometimes develop a sense of themselves as a group, a social identity or schema of who they are that is shared amongst them (Tajfel & Turner, 1986) and which contributes to the feeling of community. These group identities foster ingroup norms and resistance or opposition to outgroups (Spears & Lea, 1992). Groups may develop names for themselves, such as those in the Buffy fan group who referred to themselves as "Bronzers." As I showed in *Tune In, Log On*, the soap fans in r.a.t.s. defined themselves as intelligent and witty people, primarily women, who loved soap operas, and who had rich rewarding lives. This was a response to the dominant stereotype of soap opera fans as lazy stupid women who watched because they had nothing useful to do with their time. This group identity was rarely made explicit, only stated outright in response to trolls who attacked that self-image, as seen in this excerpt from a post responding to one such flame:

What do I know? I've only got a suma cum laude BA degree, an MS in chemistry, and in a few more than a few more months, a PHD in X-ray crystallography (that's structural bio-physical chemistry). You say you are well read, Mark? Let's discuss Sartre, Kuhn, Locke, Tolstoy, quantum vs. classical mechanics, cloning, new advances in immunosuppression and drug design, Montessori, James (Henry or William), Kierkegaard, Friedman, Piaget, classical or modern theatre, the pros and cons of recycling, the deterioration of the ozone layer, global warming, James Bay, the Alaskan wilderness crisis, hiking/climbing/camping, cycling, gourmet cooking, fitness and nutrition, or any other topic in which you may feel adept. Feel free to reply in French, German, or Spanish. Chinese or Japanese, I admit, will take me a little longer to handle.

People may also join groups because they already share a social identity. Many online groups are designed for people who share a race or ethnicity, a profession, or another affiliation. Many social network sites too are designed for specific social identities such as BlackPlanet for African Americans, Schmooze for Jewish people, Jake for gay professional men, Ravelry for knitting enthusiasts, FanNation for sports fans, Vinorati for wine buffs, or Eons for aging baby boomers. Cultural location and identification may also influence the groups and social networks people join. Although Swedes are found on Facebook and MySpace, like many countries, Sweden also has a regional site, LunarStorm, to which most Swedish youth belong. LunarStorm has parallels in Arto in Denmark, and South Korea's Cyworld.

Interpersonal relationships

Online groups provide contexts for forming one-on-one relationships, which the next two chapters will consider in more detail. These friendships and sometimes romances are made visible to the group when members post reports of having met or spent time with one another (Baym, 1995). The visible pairs of connections that form are important contributors to the sense of connectivity Rheingold (1993: 5) invoked when he famously described virtual communities as "social aggregations that emerge from the Net when enough people carry on those public discussions long enough, with sufficient human feeling, to form webs of personal relationships." Interpersonal pairs provide a social mesh that underlies and helps to connect the broader web of interconnection within the group more closely.

Networks

Thus far I've focused mostly on groups which have clear boundaries – they are located at one website or have the same mailing address. Messages go to all members. One-on-one communication is backstage, conducted through private channels such as private messaging or chat. Since the early 2000s, SNSs have become increasingly popular, staking out a middle ground between private dyadic encounters and tightly bounded group interactions. Wellman (e.g. 1988; Wellman, Quan-Haase, Boase, Chen, Hampton, & de Diaz, 2003) argues that a crucial social transformation of late modernism is a shift away from tightly bounded communities towards increasing "*networked individualism*" in which each person sits at the center of his or her own personal community.

Social network sites are designed to afford organization and access to such personalized communities. boyd and Ellison (2007) defined social network sites as "web-based services that allow individuals to (1) construct a public or semi-public profile within a bounded system, (2) articulate a list of other users with whom they share a connection, and (3) view and traverse their list of connections and those made by others within the system." In traditional (if one can use that word) online communities, messages are available to be seen by all participants in that group. In SNSs, in contrast, messages are only seen by people tied to a user's individualized network, which is a small subset of the total members of the site. The only messages available to all users are those sent by the sites themselves. To the extent that members of different people's social networks overlap and are internally organized, they may constitute groups, but social networks are egocentric and no two will be identical. Thus, no two SNS users will have access to the same set of people or messages, giving them each an experience of the site that is individualized yet overlapping with others.

Just as individuals organize themselves into networks online, so too do online groups. Recent years have seen groups increasingly distributing themselves through the internet in interconnected webs of websites, blogs, SNSs, and other domains. I call this *networked collectivism*, meaning that groups of people now network throughout the internet and related mobile media, creating a shared but distributed group identity. The fans of Swedish independent music, for example, organize themselves into clusters on music-based SNSs, blogs, news sites, other SNSs, and sites developed around individual bands (Baym, 2007).

This development has empowered members of these communities to share more kinds of media with one another, and to interact in a wider variety of ways, but also challenges many of the qualities that can make these groups cohere into something more than the sum of their parts (Baym, 2007). When there is no single shared environment, the metaphor of space quickly unravels. Communities organized through multiple sites do not feel like places. Shared practices are less likely to develop when groups are spread throughout sites, especially since each site is embedded in contexts that bring with them their own communicative traditions. Norms about what constitutes appropriate behavior may be quite different in comments on YouTube videos from how they are on fan websites. In-jokes and jargon are hard to sustain when there are many places to be inside and outside at once. The resources exchanged in supportive interactions may have to be deployed repeatedly to reach all community members, and people who hang out in some of the online spaces but not all may miss them, while those who hang out in all of them may encounter too much repetition. Identities are also harder to develop. People may frequent and play roles in some interrelated sites but not others, with the consequence that a crowd of regulars who contribute in predictable ways may be harder to find or discern. A sense of group identity may be difficult to build. Interpersonal relationships may not be as visible to others, meaning that, although they are valuable to those in the relationships, their existence may be less valuable for the coherence of the group as a whole (Baym, 2007).

Engagement with local community

It is popular to criticize online communities and SNSs. Online groups and networks have been accused of being homogeneous and too easy to leave, lessening their members' encounters with diversity (Healy, 1997). "The American mytholigization of the Internet as a community," wrote Stratton (1997: 271), "represents a nostalgic dream for a mythical early modern community which reasserts the dominance of the white, middle-class male and his cultural assumptions." These critiques posit that engagement in online community, SNSs, or any other online activity reduces engagement in other, more diverse, and (at least ideally) more meaningful, communities. This chapter turns now to whether and to what extent participation in digital interaction affects engagement with one's geographical community.

One of the defining qualities of communication technologies is that they rupture the otherwise-mandatory connection between message delivery and shared space. The ability to communicate in the absence of shared space in real time invokes fears of separation from physical reality, hence Gergen's (2002) concern about "floating worlds," Meyrowitz's (1985) worries about "no sense of place," and 100-year-old arguments that the telephone would lead to a lost sense of place (Fischer, 1992). As we lose connection to space, do we also become detached from the family, friends, and neighbors whose social support comprised communities of old and on whose interconnections civil society depends?

Testing this is not easy. Most of the data that we have about the impacts of digital media on people's local connections comes from surveys, many of which divide users into categories based on whether or not they use the internet or how much they use it in comparison to one another. There are serious theoretical problems with both these strategies. They assume that simply using the internet or using it more than others may cause effects, regardless of how it is used (Campbell & Kwak, in press; Jung et al., 2001). Nie and Erbring (2000) defined "regular users" as those who use the internet five or more hours a week, yet offered no explanation for what is magical about five hours that makes it more different from four than from six (Jung et al., 2001). Why would we expect the person who spends six hours a week online playing poker to experience the same social consequences as someone who spends her six online hours each week keeping in touch with distant relatives, arranging community events, and reading political blogs? Furthermore, proficient users who are at ease with the technology may take less time to accomplish the same activities online or with a mobile telephone (Campbell & Kwak, in press; Jung et al., 2001). It's not surprising, given these measures, that the results of studies are mixed. As a whole, though, they do not support the dystopian critique that time spent online detracts from social life offline. The roles of the internet in civic and political engagement are vast and well beyond the scope of this book (see, e.g., Dahlgren, 2005, 2009; Hartelius, 2005), so consider what follows to be a cursory look.

Civic engagement

One way to assess civic engagement is to ask people how many of their neighbors they know. Katz and Rice (2002) compared people who had used the internet recently to non-users of the internet and found that recent users knew the fewest, while non-users were most likely to know them all. On the other hand, in a study of a suburb of Toronto built to be wired from the ground up, Hampton and Wellman (2003) found that those who had the high-speed access when they moved in had three times the local connections and communicated more with neighbors both online and offline. They also stayed in touch more with long-distance friends and relatives who continued to provide them social support that the non-wired residents did not have (Wellman et al., 2003).

When the internet is used to connect neighbors, it can enhance their connections to one another and to their communities. Hampton (in press) wrote that there are more than 10,000 neighborhood groups in Yahoo!'s group directories, one of many sites that offer neighbors the means to connect. In a study of a neighborhood email list in Israel, Mesch and Levanon (2003) found that the list increased the size of people's local networks and extended their participation in the community. In his "I-Neighbors" project, Hampton (in press) provided all online Americans with the means to create online groups for their neighborhoods and then studied those groups. People created over 6,000 neighborhoods, although 80 percent only attracted 1 or 2 participants. But 28 percent of the most active neighborhoods were disadvantaged communities. People used these groups to organize local activities such as cleaning up the yards of elderly neighbors. Hampton concluded that the internet has the potential to increase the collective efficacy of those who are economically and structurally disadvantaged.

In choosing the decline of bowling leagues to epitomize the decline of community in American life, Putnam emphasized engagement in clubs and organizations as a means of assessing civic engagement. Surveys by Cole (2000), Katz and Rice (2002), and Katz and Aspden (1997) compared internet users and non-users in terms of their engagement with clubs and volunteer organizations. Though differences were small, internet users reported spending more time with such civic associations. In one of the few studies looking at mobile phone use and civic engagement, Campbell and Kwak (2009) polled a stratified sample of Americans chosen to reflect their representativeness vis-à-vis census data. People who used mobile phones to exchange information and opinions were more likely to "do volunteer work, work on a community project, contribute money to a social group or cause, go to a community or neighborhood meeting, and [work] on behalf of a social group or cause." Echoing the discussion from chapter 1 about the importance of skill in understanding issues of access, Campbell and Kwak found that using the mobile phone for civic purposes was more likely when people were comfortable with the technology. This implies that designing technologies for ease of use is an important factor in enabling their use for civic purposes.

One can argue that the increases in public wifi and mobile phone use mean that people are less engaged with their physical environments and hence less likely to engage the diverse people in public realms. In an observational and interview study of four public parks with wifi in two countries (the USA and Canada), Hampton, Livio, and Sessions (in press) found that wifi users did pay less attention to their surroundings. They kept their heads down and hence closed themselves off to interaction with others in the park. However, when asked, 28 percent of them said that they had met a stranger in that park, and most were actively engaged with other people through their wifi connections.

Political engagement

Critics warn that "real" political engagement, the kind that gets people out of their chairs and into the streets organizing and acting, may be replaced by "virtual" engagement, in which reading political blogs and chatting politics online provides an illusion of political engagement. "Simulated activism is no substitute for the real thing," wrote Hartelius (2005), summarizing this critique. As we saw in chapter 2, concerns about authenticity are endemic to the reception of new media. But some evidence suggests that people who use digital media may be more likely to be politically engaged offline than those who do not. Internet users have been found to be more likely than non-users to engage in political activities, read magazines and newspapers, attend to campaign coverage in TV shows and interviews, and, perhaps most importantly, vote (Katz & Rice, 2002). Campbell and Kwak (in press) found that when people used their mobile phones to discuss and exchange opinions on issues, they were also more likely to "attend a political meeting, rally, or speech, circulate a petition for a candidate or issue, and to contact a public official or political party."

A 2008 survey of Americans by the Pew Internet and American Life Project (Smith, Schlozman, Verba, & Brady, 2009) found that 19 percent of internet-using adults (14 percent of all American adults) "have posted material about political or social issues or used a social networking site for some form of civic or political engagement." Those who did this online, like those who did it offline, were considerably more affluent and educated than those who did not. Smith et al. also found that the people who used the internet politically were "much more likely to be invested in other forms of civic and political activism." Pew's survey found half of the adults who posted content online about political or social issues had contacted a government official, 61 percent had signed a petition, 22 percent had sent a letter to the editor, and 81 percent had made a charitable contribution. These percentages are considerably higher than they are among adults as a whole, and dramatically higher than they are for those who do not go online at all.

We are also seeing new media being used in novel ways to engage people in the political process. Twitter has emerged as a means for people to organize flash mobs in order to protest. In 2009, political protests in Macedonia were organized quickly through Twitter. Twitter was banned in the country shortly thereafter, indicating the extent to which it was seen as a powerful tool for political action rather than a substitute for real action. The use of YouTube to enable citizens to pose questions in the 2008 US presidential debates is another important example.

Even if one grants that political activity online is real, there is a concern that political interaction through new media serves to polarize opinions rather than facilitating discussion across diverse viewpoints. This is in keeping with the critique that online communities are homogeneous and limit exposure to diversity. Gergen (2008) speculates that people are increasingly engaged in "monadic clusters," small groups that affirm one another's perspective and lead people away from political action. Anyone reading opposing political blogs cannot help but be struck by the sense of parallel worlds, in which the same events have completely different and irreconcilable meanings. My local newspaper, the *Lawrence Journal-World*, has an online version where people can post comments on articles. The discussion there is lively and active (more than 1,000,000 comments have been posted), and diverse perspectives are raised. Repeated reading, however, shows that the discourse is polarized and the comment threads serve more to solidify opinions and divide readers into camps than to facilitate a new middle ground. Campbell and Kwak (2009) found that the monadic cluster effect holds best when people are in small diverse social networks. When communication happens in a small social circle of people who disagree, individuals are more apt to opt out of political discussion and engagement rather than risk the peace. However, in large social networks and in small ones marked by similarity, mobile phone use to discuss issues was associated with increased political participation.

The many complex ways in which engagement in digital inter-action impact civic and political life are not yet clear. New media may inspire more political activity amongst those who use them. They may polarize publics and make the meaningful compromise necessary for governance in diverse societies increasingly difficult to attain. They may also offer disenfranchised groups new potential to organize for change.

Summary

In closing this chapter, let's return to the key concepts and theoretical perspectives identified in the first two chapters. New technologies offer many affordances that influence what happens through and because of them. Their combination of interac-tivity and reach allow people to come together around shared interests, transcending local communities in ways that may be personally empowering but potentially polarizing. Asynchronous platforms in particular offer people access to like-minded others and support, whether those others are online simultaneously or not. Synchronous or near-synchronous platforms like Twitter, combined with broad reach and replicability, can enable swift grassroots organizing. Minimal social cues in some online groups can open doors for people to make riskier self-disclosures, and hence to gain more social support, but may also contribute to polarization, as people may feel less pressured to find peaceful middle grounds. The mobility of many new media helps them to be concretely tied to location even as people move around, and can hence support local civic engagement.

Technological determinism might predict either that these combinations of features usher in a new era in which people substitute simulated communities for real ones or that they are democratizing, empowering people to participate and increasing civic engagement. Social constructivism would focus on the social forces that influence community online and off, including the social identities of people who participate, the motivations that inspire their online actions, and the social norms they develop around how to behave and what counts as skill and competence. Social shaping and domestication approaches would do as this chapter has, looking at both the technological factors and the social ones that combine unpredictably to create practices and outcomes that have not yet cohered into clear consequences. What does seem clear at this point is that new media do not offer inauthentic simulations that detract from or substitute for real engagement. As we will continue to see in the remaining chapters, what happens through mediation is interwoven, not juxtaposed, with everything else.

5

New relationships, new selves?

Tom was a sweet and thoughtful guy who took my class about online interaction in the mid 1990s. In one paper, he explored what would happen if he represented himself in different ways through his America Online profile. He created one profile as a stereotypically sexy young woman who described herself as liking fast cars she didn't know much about and liking men who did. Within hours of logging in as "Busty," he had received dozens of personal messages inviting him backstage for some quick cybersex. It was his first experience of the receiving end of sexism and, though it wasn't hard for some of us to see it coming, it left him aghast. Some months later, he decided he was ready to find committed romance. His friend advised him that the best strategy was to log onto America Online and search the profiles for women in the city who were online and shared his interests, then send them a private message. He took the advice, combined it with the lesson he had learned as Busty ("treat women as people"), and quickly fell into an exchange of messages with a woman who lived nearby but whom he'd never met. The chat progressed so well that, within a couple of hours, she gave him her phone number and told him to call. He called immediately and they spoke on the phone for an hour before she suggested that they meet for dinner that night. She brought friends, just in case he turned out to be a psychokiller. He wasn't, their chemistry was undeniable, and by day's end they were en route to their eventual marriage. Though they had met in person the same day they met online, when her family attended his graduation ceremony, one commented "wow, you really were a graduate student!" Because they had met online, some in her family still doubted his honesty.

Tom's story encapsulates the utopian potential the internet

holds for our relationships – we can meet new people and form rewarding new relationships – as well as the common concerns that the people we meet online cannot be trusted and may even be dangerous. Busty could be Tom. Tom could be a fraud or even a killer. When the telegraph took off, operators working in telegraph offices soon found that the time between customers was well spent using the technology to chat with telegraph operators in other offices in the network. As Standage (1998) recounts, this led to the formation of new relationships, many of which were regarded with suspicion by the relational partners' families and peers. In chapter 2, we saw that, throughout the history of electronic communication, some have celebrated the ability to form new relationships across time and space, but others have seen it as enabling communication between people who should not be forming relationships and as offering pale substitutes for authentic connection. The internet has been heralded for its potential to bridge divides and create meaningful new connections, but more often accused of leading people to lie about themselves, making victims of women and children, or taking people away from the relationships they should be having with their families and communities.

Initially, most of the focus in both the popular imagination and internet scholarship was on the development of new relationships between strangers who met through the internet. In this chapter and the next we will look at the processes of forming new relationships through the internet. This chapter focuses on first meeting new people online. After discussing how and why people form new relationships through the internet, I turn to the questions of identity, asking what forces shape people's online self-presentations and whether they are more likely to be honest or deceptive. Finally, the chapter returns to the question of authenticity, asking whether the identities and new connections people construct online are as real as those built offline.

New relationships online

The internet has brought to all of its users the possibility of forming relationships that transcend space. As shared location has lost its status as a prerequisite for first meeting, the range of potential relational partners has been expanded to a broader pool than at any previous point in history. Most often, relationships emerge naturally out of the online communities and networks we discussed in the previous chapter. In the soap opera discussion forum I studied, rec.arts.tv.soaps (r.a.t.s.), many friendships developed in the course of talking about soap operas and the tangents that discussion prompted. Participants often described the group as "a bunch of close friends" (Baym, 2000). This was typical for newsgroups. In the early 1990s, Parks and Floyd (1996) sampled 24 Usenet newsgroups and then emailed a survey to a sampling of people who had posted to each group. They found that 60.7 percent of respondents had established a personal relationship of some sort through the group, regardless of what kind of group it was. In a follow-up survey of MOO participants, Parks and Roberts (1998) found that so many respondents had formed personal relationships through MOOs that there weren't enough people left over without such relationships to use for comparison.

Although people mainly use social network sites (SNSs) to maintain existing relationships (as we'll cover in the next chapter), they are sites of new relationship formation as well. Haythornthwaite (2002) coined the term "latent tie" to refer to potential relationships within a social circle that are structurally enabled but have not been activated. Friends of friends on Facebook are a good example of latent ties and a source of new relationships. By making friends' lists visible and, in some cases, offering automated recommendations of latent ties, the architecture of social network sites facilitates the conversion of latent ties to acquaintanceships (Ellison et al., 2007).

People may also explicitly seek new partners online, which accounts for the rise of dating sites such as eHarmony.com and Match.com, as well as start-ups like omegle.com, a chat platform that randomly pairs strangers for real-time interaction. Match making is not new to digital media. Newspapers have long hosted classified ads for those seeking romance and, in alternative publications, playmates. When media become "marriage market intermediaries" they blur interpersonal and mass communication

(Adelman & Ahuvia, 1991). Ideologies of romanticism, in which true love arises out of unpredictable moments of serendipitous fate, are pitted against ideologies of social exchange in which finding love through media seems more of a business transaction than destiny and people are reduced to dehumanizing lists of attributes (Adelman & Ahuvia, 1991).

There are many reasons people might form new relationships online even when they don't go looking for them, including the communication imperative, assumed similarity, and reduced social risk. Regardless of medium, people are intrinsically motivated to reduce our uncertainty about others and find affinities with them (Walther, 1992). Walther (1992) proposed the Social Information Processing (SIP) model to explain relational development online. In his 1992 piece and in Walther et al. (1994: 465), he argued that, because people need to reduce uncertainty, in online contexts they "adapt their linguistic and textual behaviors to the solicitation and presentation of socially revealing, relational behavior." The longer the interaction lasts or the more expectation the participants have of continued interaction, the more true this is (Walther, 1994).

When people are in a discussion forum based on common interest, there is a presumption of similarity which can make potential partners seem more attractive. "When someone joins a newsgroup devoted to, for example, aging ferrets," write McKenna et al. (2002: 11), "he or she already knows that there is a shared base of interest with the others there." Similarity functions as a form of propinquity (Baker, 2008). Online, we bump into the people who share our interests rather than those who happen to be in the same physical location. This leads to connections that might not otherwise form. The internet also lowers the social risk of communicating. We saw this, for example, in last chapter's discussion of McKenna and Bargh's (1998) work on newsgroups for homosexuals and will return to it later in this chapter. Just as people spill their secrets to strangers seated beside them on airplanes, the anonymity of online interactions makes some people more willing to disclose and fosters new relationship formation.

Given these advantages of new media, one could imagine a world in which they are wholeheartedly embraced as a wonderful opportunity. But shared location has been intrinsic to our under-standings of how relationships start and their place in our personal networks for millennia. We are most likely to form relationships with those with whom we get the chance to interact, and, without communication technology, those are the people who are most likely to be in the same place at the same time. In substituting interest or other factors for place, mediated meeting challenges much of what we've taken for granted in forming relationships for most of human history.

Mediated meeting also challenges our conventional understand-ings of relationship building because we are used to assessing people and doing much of the work of getting closer through nonverbal signals. We often size people up and decide whether or not to talk to them based on how they look. At least in romantic relationships, people may be most motivated to pursue connec-tions with those whose level of physical attractiveness matches their own, a phenomenon known as the "matching hypothesis" (Berscheid, Dion, Hatfield, & Walster, 1971). In online contexts, we may be unaware of what our communication partner looks like, or may not find out until well into the relationship. Even when there are photographs, they may be carefully selected to present one's best look rather than one's everyday appearance. Once a relation-ship has begun, nonverbal cues are important in its development. We smile, make eye contact, stand closer and touch to signal attrac-tion and deepen our bonds (e.g. Knapp, 1983). How then can we form relationships in the absence of such nonverbal messages? And what are the consequences of doing so?

One answer, as we saw in the third chapter, is that even text-based new media afford many ways to express emotion. We use emoticons to signal friendliness, we use punctuation and capi-talization to insert feeling, we use informal language and talk-like phonetic spellings to create an air of conversationality. Multimedia platforms let us share video and engage in real-time video chat. We use language to talk about our feelings. Socioemotional communi-cation may be easier face to face, but it is common and successful in digital media as well. In one of his SIP studies, Walther (1994) conducted experiments with groups who had never met. They were told either that this was a one-shot meeting or that they would be interacting again in the future. When people expected to interact again they were more likely to express immediacy and affection, similarity and depth, trust and composure.

Another reason for societal discomfort with online relationship formation is that these new relationships are often between categories of people who would not have as much of a chance to form relationships offline. People communicating in different locations, relying on textual and digital nonverbal cues, are more likely to form relationships that blur the social boundaries between groups and hence challenge social norms of appropriateness. This is another way in which new relationship formation online challenges conventional notions of what relationships are and should be. New media make it easier to have "pure relationships," in which the relationship is its own reward instead of serving a useful function in maintaining the social order (Clark, 1998; Giddens, 1993). Standage (1998) wrote of then-shocking interracial relationships that emerged through the telegraph, as well as of romances formed without parental consent and over parental objections. One couple was even married by telegraph in distant locations to avert the marriage the bride's father had planned for her. Though her father challenged the marriage's authenticity, given that the couple were not co-located during the ceremony, it was upheld by the courts.

Friendships between women and men are more common in online contexts. Offline, these relationships are generally seen as a threat to the social order (e.g. Rawlins, 1992). In English they are described with the term "just friends," betraying the cultural definition of such relationships as something less than would be expected of a man and a woman. Parks and Roberts (1998) surveyed users of seven MOOs by contacting them directly and asking them to describe a recent person with whom they had communicated recently on the site and to compare that relationship to an offline relationship. They found far more cross-sex friendships in MOOs than face to face. In a survey of users of the international music-oriented SNS Last.fm, I asked people to describe a random on-site friendship. Relationships on Last.fm were as likely to be cross-sex as same-sex, making the former more common on Last. fm than offline (Baym & Ledbetter, 2009). In a survey of nearly 1,000 Israeli teens, Mesch and Talmud (2006) also found more cross-sex relationships between online than offline friends.

Relationships that transcend age barriers may also be more common online (Mesch & Talmud, 2006), although we did not find this to be the case on Last.fm (Baym & Ledbetter, 2009). People in their forties and teenagers who share guild member- ship in online role-playing games may become friends; people who share musical taste may connect without even knowing one another's age in music-oriented sites and groups; television fans may bond over shows regardless of age. When cross-sex and cross- age friends interact online, they are less likely to face the pressures of others' (and, for some, their own) suspicions than they are if they socialize face to face. These relationships may thus be easier to create and maintain online than off.

Identity

Flexibility and multiplicity

Without doubt, the issues that shake people the most about forming relationships online center on identity. When people's bodies aren't visible, will people lie about who they are? Can they be known? Can they be trusted? Can the relationships they form be valid? Alternatively, might some be liberated? An *Off the Mark* cartoon by Mark Parisi (2009), titled "Life before the internet," echoed many of the concerns we saw in cartoons and advice columns in chapter 2. In the cartoon, an unattractive man sat before a desk with nothing on it. "I'm pretending to be handsome," said the thought bubble over his head, "Yup, athletic too . . . Now I'm pretending to be a woman."

Many scholars have noted that digital media, especially the internet, disrupt the notion held dear in many cultures that each body gets one self (e.g. Stone, 1995). Digital media seem to sepa- rate selves from bodies, leading to *disembodied identities* that exist only in actions and words. This disembodiment opens up new possibilities for exploration and deception. People can certainly lie in person, but it is hard (though by no means impossible) to pretend to be the other sex or a different age. Many academic reports in the early 1990s focused on Multi-User Domains (MUDs) and MOOs in which much of the point was to play with identity. However, observational research showed that, even in those environments where people could self-present as anything from a monster to a six-pack of beer, most people did not take advantage of disembodiment to create fantastic or radically deceptive selves (Curtis, 1997).

The disembodied identities presented online can also be multiple. On Last.fm, for instance, I am Popgurl, a self-representation I took great pains to keep separate from Nancy Baym for some time before publicly claiming her. In the fan board discussing my favorite band, I used my cat's name, not because I didn't want the others in the group to know who I am, but because I didn't want that fangirl to show up when people search for this academic on Google. A search for Nancy Baym will turn up my academic persona on my university website, a more well-rounded if trite self-presentation on Twitter, and a more pop-culture-oriented self on my blog. All of these are genuine parts of me, but online they are segmented into separate spaces where they can become distinct identities. My son, well socialized by educators to believe it's dangerous to reveal his underage status or identifying information online, maintains several different identities with different names, ages, and locations in different sites on the internet.

Such multiplicity is enhanced on the internet, but it is nothing new. It was Shakespeare who wrote that "all the world's a stage," recognizing that all of our social encounters involve playing roles designed to suit the interactants and the context. Identity scholars such as Goffman (1959) have long argued that the self plays multiple roles in everyday life and cannot be understood adequately as a single unified entity. Rather than there being One True Self, variations of which are inherently false, contemporary scholars have come to see the self as flexible and multiple, taking different incarnations in different situations. Finkenauer, Engels, Meeus, and Oosterwegel (2002: 28), for instance, defined identity as representing "the aspect of the self that is accessible and salient in a particular context and that interacts with the environment." Turkle (1996: 14) used the metaphor of windows. If you think of a computer screen, an internet user may have multiple windows open. In one, he is playing a warlock in a role-playing game; in another he is chatting with his best friend in another town; in a third, he is working on homework; in yet another, he's drafting an email to his parents; and in a fifth, he's in a chat room pretending to be a woman. "Windows have become a powerful metaphor for thinking about the self as a multiple, distributed system," Turkle writes; "The self is no longer simply playing different roles in different settings at different times. The life practice of windows is that of a decentered self that exists in many worlds, that plays many roles at the same time." Now the embodied self, as one of Turkle's interviewees put it, may be "just one more window."

Knowing bodies is often seen as key to knowing individuals, to determining whether their actions are valid, and to holding them accountable for what they do (Stone, 1995). When there's no body attached to behavior, the authenticity of behavior becomes less clear. It took a nineteenth-century court to determine that the marriage ceremony conducted via telegraph counted as real despite the lack of co-presence and the bride's father's objections (Standage, 1998). Consider the example of the "cyberaffairs" we saw cited repeatedly in the advice columns of the American 1990s as one of the internet's worst relational consequences. For the letter writers, there was no question such relationships were affronts to their marriages, but whether they constitute adultery is less clear. Divorce courts increasingly deliberate cases in which one partner has been accused of "adultery" for an "affair" carried on through the verbal description of sex acts with a partner online. Most of us may feel betrayed were this to happen in our relationships, but does a sex act count as a sex act without bodies? Can it be adultery if they never physically touched? The problem of what kinds of realities are warranted by online behaviors are by no means limited to sex. What about when an avatar "steals" a digital object in an online role-playing game? Is that really theft? Can the person playing the stealing avatar be held accountable in real-world courts of law (a question addressed in Charles Stross's 2007 novel *Halting State*, where authorities were initially reluctant to intervene in a bank robbery conducted within a role-playing game)? We don't yet have clear strategies to think through the actions of personas that may be distinct from those in the bodies that type those behaviors.

Cues and competence

Online, as in all media and face to face interaction, we try to manage what other people think of us (Goffman, 1959). This impression management may involve outright deception, total honesty, or, most often, a strategic balance of sharing, withholding, and distorting information. Our ability to construct an online identity, whether authentic, fanciful, or manipulative is limited and enabled by the communicative tools, or affordances, a platform makes available and our skill at strategically managing them. In this section, we'll see how we use these cues to build a personal, individualized, identity and to align ourselves with other social groups.

Personal identity

In many online environments, people seek to individualize themselves as different from the other participants. Different kinds of sites and media provide different cues that can facilitate this. In Farside MUD, a fantasy environment, high-level players could purchase genitalia in order to make their avatars sexually mature (Ito, 1997). In MOOs like those discussed in the last chapter, there may be multiple gender identities from which to choose (Danet, 1998). In graphic role-playing games, identities are often created through costumes, weapons, and levels of skill. In a role-playing game like Runescape, which is particularly popular amongst boys in early adolescence, it takes a considerable investment of time and requires a high level of competence to build an identity by collecting the right clothes and weapons, and constructing an impressive in-game dwelling. In Club Penguin, a popular site for children, kids build identities by purchasing their own igloo which they can decorate with the furniture they choose. They can also choose their clothes and may even adopt a Pet Puffle. Not all digital environments are so creative, but all provide us with options for self-presentation. On mailing lists and web boards, our signature files, choices of name, and even our domain names become important markers of who we are.

The most important identity signal may be one's name. An authentic name may be required for trust. Most email providers, web boards, blogs, and SNSs allow users to select any name. On Last.fm, it is unusual to see a real name. Korea's Cyworld, on the other hand, allows people to pick pseudonyms only after their identity has been verified and "the site's search functions are able to validate the name, date of birth, and gender of other users" (Kim & Yun, 2007). Facebook requires real names. One analysis of 4,540 Facebook profiles of students at Carnegie Mellon University (USA) (Gross & Acquisti, 2005) found that 89 percent of user names seemed to be real. Only 8 percent were clearly false and just 3 percent partial; 80 percent had pictures that made them identifiable. However, Facebook's system for recognizing authenticity is flawed, resulting in multiple profiles bearing the names of celebrities, businesses, or websites. "If this rule is being followed," jokes Baron (2008: 82), "then Karl Marx, Anne Boleyn, and Kermit the Frog are alive and well."

In textual media, the use of written language is a significantly more powerful force in making and forming impressions than it is when people interact body to body. While physically attractive people may be the ones who get noticed at a party, it's often the articulate, insightful and witty ones who know how to spell who gain notice at the online equivalent. Language is also our primary tool for telling others about ourselves through self-disclosure. As we'll discuss in the next chapter, self-disclosure is indispensable in turning strangers into relational partners and to maintaining ongoing relationships. Its strategic management is essential to shaping the impressions others form of us.

The images we associate with ourselves, including our photographs and avatars are also important identity cues. On Facebook, people usually use photographs of themselves as identifiers. On Last.fm, in contrast, avatar pictures rarely depict the users, just as users rarely use real names. The appeal of those pictures alone may lead to the initiation of new relationships, as Last.fm users told me when I asked them about how they came to friend the people they did (Baym & Ledbetter, 2009).

Websites and blogs provide spaces to use language, but they provide many other potential identity cues. This makes technical competence in cue manipulation particularly important. We need to know how to make the blank slate of a web page into something meaningful. Knowledge of language and spelling matters, but so too does facility with html and CSS. In a content analysis of 1,000 homepages from four different networks, Papacharissi (2002) found that many people tried to display an image of technological competence. Some displayed "what ranged from uncontrolled enthusiasm to blatant exhibitionism," while those "much more proficient in Web design displayed this savvy by avoiding the mass produced templates, animations, and other 'recipes,' and asserting their individuality and creativity with original HTML code" (Papacharissi, 2002: 656).

One of the unique qualities of most SNSs is that they engineer self-presentation by providing predetermined sets of categories through which to build identities. Though the categories vary, most provide slots for demographic information including age, place of residence, and general interests. Lampe, Ellison, and Steinfeld (2007) used automated data collection to gather profile information from all available profiles on their university's Facebook system and found that, on average, users filled in 59 percent of fields available to them. Gross and Acquisti (2005) found that 98.5 percent of their university's Facebook users disclosed their full birthdates. General-interest categorizations encourage users to construct themselves in part by identifying with popular culture. The early SNS, Friendster, offered five categories (general interests, music, movies, television, and books) which are also used on MySpace, Facebook, and Orkut (Liu, 2007). This kind of categorization of the self began in online dating sites (Fiore & Donath, 2005), the assumption being that people who share such tastes are likely to be interpersonally compatible and hence good prospects for relational success. On Last.fm, we found that friends were more likely than not to share musical taste, but the extent to which a Last. fm relationship was motivated by the other person's taste in music and a shared musical history did not predict how developed their relationship was (Baym & Ledbetter, 2009). Taste lists also provide a way to perform our individuality by differentiating ourselves from others (Liu, 2007). Liu (2007) examined 127,477 MySpace profiles and found that "on average, MySpace users tended to differentiate themselves from their friends, rather than identifying with their friends' tastes," perhaps in order to distinguish themselves from the other people in their social circles.

Social identity

Self-presentations online are built of all of these cues as we appropriate them in the service of crafting our identities. Some see online identities as free-floating in this space, and see our use of cues as a potential act of pure self-reinvention. But, far from free-floating, even online, our identities are entwined with the identities of others. Individual identities are deeply enmeshed with social identities. We build self-representations by linking to others. Others also contribute to the online pool of information available about ourselves. We also indicate our membership in social groups that invoke shared conceptions of insider and outsider.

We link to others in many ways. On blogs, homepages, and other sites, people use links that send messages about who they are and with whom they seek to be affiliated. Those links serve as elements of our representation, and the behavior of and impressions left by those others become elements in the mix, shaping how people are perceived. In an analysis of homepages, Wynn and Katz (1998) found that identities constructed through homepages were richly contextualized in offline social groups through self-descriptions, implied audiences, and links to web-sites of other people and groups. When links to others require the others' acceptance, as is the case in many SNSs, the sheer number of links a person has can be a status marker. People may be evaluated by how many friends they have (boyd, 2006; Fono and Raynes-Goldie, 2006).

One of the unique affordances of SNSs is that they display friend lists, making everyone's connections visible to at least some others. Donath and boyd (2004: 72) were among the first to note that displaying one's connection carries potential risk to one's reputation, writing that "[s]eeing someone within the context of their connections provides the viewer with information about them. Social status, political beliefs, musical taste, etc., may be inferred from the company one keeps." Whatever one writes within a profile may be supported or undermined by one's visible connections. On SNSs our friends' names, words, and even looks can influence others' impressions of us. Walther et al. (2008) had one group evaluate the attractiveness of people's photos. They then created fake Facebook profiles to display photos of friends with varying degrees of attractiveness and had another set of subjects evaluate the profiles. The same people were rated as more attractive when they had better-looking Facebook friends, and less attractive when they had links to unattractive people.

Friends can also affect one's image by writing on one's "wall" or "shoutbox" (Walther et al., 2008), tagging photographs with one's name, and commenting on content one has uploaded. In some SNSs, people can do this even if they have not been accepted as a friend. "This makes participative social networking technologies different from Web pages, e-mail, or online chat," Walther et al. write (2008: 29), "because all those technologies allow the initiator complete control over what appears in association with his- or herself." Content posted by others may contribute disproportionately to one's image because it may be seen as less biased by a desire to look good.

The self-representations we create are far from the only source of information available about us online, and most people who become interested in learning about an individual will turn to search engines where, if anything comes up at all, it is likely to be a mix of what the person has put online and information placed there by others (and sometimes about others who share the same name). People may post information about us, tag us in photographs, link to us, and discuss us, and all of these uncontrollable bits of information about our identities may come up in searches whether we wish they did or not.

Different media platforms provide differing cues for building shared social and cultural identities. Whether, and how, a user can construct a racial identity will vary considerably from site to site. In her analysis of BlackPlanet.com, Byrne (2007) reports that, until 2005, members' only choices for racial identification were Black, Asian, Latino, Native American, and White. Following Nakamura (2002), she argues this "forces users into dominant notions of race," leaving little room for intercultural diversity or intraracial identities. Other SNSs, such as MySpace, Last.fm, or Facebook, do not provide any category for race, which, one might argue, reflects an effort to render race irrelevant or, following Silver (2000), an assumption that the users, like most of the developers, are White.

Like race, nationality can be a charged identity category and platforms differ in whether and how they foreground it. We saw in chapter 3 that nations vary dramatically in the extent to which they are represented online, and that English-speaking nations are disproportionately present. On-site cultures emerge around national identities. Last.fm used to display all users' nationality if they'd selected it from a drop-down list of options, leading to some distress from people such as Scots, some of whom did not self-identify as residents of the United Kingdom (which was provided in the drop-down menu), but of Scotland (which was not).The most striking example of this is Orkut (Fragoso, 2006). Orkut, owned by Google, launched as a US-based SNS in 2004. People could join only when invited by an existing member. Within a short time, Brazilians outnumbered every other country's members, a phenomenon which usually has been attributed to Brazilians' purported sociable and outgoing nature, an explanation which is surely inadequate (Fragoso, 2006). People on Orkut began to construct their identities in terms of nationalism, leading to intense conflicts that were often grounded in language wars as Portuguese speakers colonized what had been English-language discussion groups.

In international contexts, claiming a national identity can be a way of differentiating one's self. Miller and Slater's (2000) interviews with Trinidadians about their internet use described Trinis as often surprised to realize that the strangers they met from other countries online had not heard of their country. They responded by seeking to represent Trinidad as part of their own identities online, acting as nationalistic selves. They filled their homepages with links to official Trini sites, and, as we discussed in chapter 3, replicated norms of the Trini speech community in their online interactions.

Even when race, nationality, or other social identities are not explicit, they may be imputed from cues such as the taste selections on one's SNS profile or the interests one displays. Our vocabulary choices may reveal our age or nationality. It's not hard, for instance, to spot the British on Twitter when they use terms such as "bollocks." Tastes and interests are shaped by socioeconomic factors, including money, class, and education, as well as by age and locational cohorts (Bourdieu, 1984; Liu, 2007). Digital identity cues are "signals of social position in an information based society" (Donath, 2007).

According to the Social Identity Theory of Deindividuation Effects, or SIDE Model, the extent to which people identify and behave in accordance with social rather than personal identities is influenced by the medium's affordances, such as anonymity, which interact with social context, and social understandings of the self (e.g. Spears & Lea, 1992). In a series of experiments manipulating the extent to which people in online groups were connected and given varying amounts of information that served to anonymize, individualize, or invoke social identities for participants, Lea, Spears, and their collaborators (e.g. Lea & Spears, 1991) found that, when people have access to individualizing cues, they are more likely to differentiate themselves from one another. In anonymous contexts, however, people are more likely to stereotype and conform to group norms, experiencing more of a sense of "we" and less a sense of "me." This stereotyping extends to our own self-perceptions and behaviors (Postmes & Baym, 2005). Thus, for instance, fans of University of Kansas athletics (the Jayhawks) participating in online forums where their status as a Jayhawk is foregrounded over individualizing social cues are likely to engage in behaviors such as saying nasty things about rivals University of Missouri (the Tigers) and all those affiliated with them. The same individuals, participating in groups that emphasize their individualized identities or shared social identity as Midwestern college students, might be less likely to present themselves as Jayhawks or Tigers and, as a result, get along just fine.

Honesty

I began this chapter with the pervasive idea that people met online may not be trustworthy. As we have seen throughout this book, people often expect others to be less honest online. At one extreme, people are taken to invent entire new disembodied identities. They may also be seen as modestly tweaking themselves around the margins. To the extent online self-representations are grounded in explicit connections with identifiable others, as I have just been discussing, it is difficult to create online selves that wander too far from the embodied ones. On SNSs, where people often identify themselves with real names, new people are usually encountered because they are latent ties (Haythornthwaite, 2002) – people with at least one common on-site friend – and are hence more likely to be trusted. As we will see, though, people may fudge the truth on those sites as well.

One might not be surprised that people are pressured toward honesty in SNSs, yet still expect that, in other more anonymous online environments, people would be less honest. In general, the idea that anonymity makes people lie has not been well supported by the research. Rutter and Smith (1999) studied over 17,000 messages in an online newsgroup, and found that fantasy selves were rare. In r.a.t.s, group norms encouraged honest self-presentation (Baym, 2000). Though people may have tinkered with their self-presentations around the edges, only one person, who insisted he was the nephew of the fictional soap opera character Aunt Phoebe, was discernibly deceptive during my three years in the site. New users with anonymous usernames were regularly asked to share their real names and a little about themselves so we could get to know them better. In-depth interviews with a small sample of users of chat rooms (Henderson & Gilding, 2004) showed that the interviewees focused on the continuities rather than the differences between online and offline relationships, and described high rates of honest self-disclosure in both.

Whether anonymous or identifiable, people seem at least as likely to be more honest online than off. Reduced social cues make it easier to lie, but separation, time lags, and sparse cues also remove social pressures that make lying seem a good idea. When we can't be seen and can easily log off and change screen names, we don't have to face the consequences of disclosures gone wrong. When the people with whom we're interacting online don't know any of the same people that we do offline, word won't get around (McKenna et al., 2002). The sense of safety in anonymous sites may be important for honest self-expression. This can also be important for those who are socially anxious and lonely or who have stigmatized identities. McKenna and her collaborators (2002) emailed a survey to every fifth poster in a sample of 20 Usenet newsgroups. They found that people who were socially anxious or lonely were more likely to feel they could express their real selves online, and this was positively correlated with developing relationships online that led to other media and offline meetings. Even when interacting with those who know us, the ability to write out one's thoughts and not have to face the other immediately can lead to more honesty. Americans report being more honest with loved ones through email than face to face (Rainie, Lenhart, Fox, Spooner, & Horrigan, 2000).

Testing out honest self-disclosure and expressing one's "real" self online can be empowering and liberating. Practicing skills such as assertiveness can help people to work through issues involving control and mastery, gain competence, and find a comfort which they can then transfer to their embodied encounters. This is especially so when they receive positive feedback for their online expressions of identity (McKenna & Bargh, 1998; Myers, 1987b; Turkle, 1996, 1997). Gay teenagers, for instance, may first come out in online communities focused on gay identity. Finding an accepting cohort helps them to feel at ease with acknowledging their homosexuality, giving them the confidence to tell their family and peers offline (McKenna & Bargh, 1998; see also Gray, 2009). The socially anxious people McKenna et al. (2002) studied formed new close relationships through the internet and reported less loneliness and greater ease making friends offline two years later. The power people may feel when given the mediated affordance of greater cue control extends beyond computer mediation. In a prescient article, Sarch (1993) interviewed women about their use of the telephone in dating relationships and found that having control over the cues they conveyed to their male partners gave them a greater sense of power in the developing relationship.

It would be naïve to imagine that people do not deceive online. With the rare and well-publicized exception, however, most lies told through the wonders of technology's affordances are minor strategic manipulations rather than malevolent falsehoods. Whitty and Gavin (2001) trained their students to conduct interviews with people who regularly used the internet in their study of online relational development. These 60 interviews showed that people were worried about honesty, and with good reason. Men and women offered different reasons for deception. Women who lied generally did so for safety reasons. The men rarely reported that rationale; they were, however, more likely to report that the internet's anonymity made them feel more able to disclose honestly. Whitty and Gavin conclude that "the ideals that are important in traditional relationships, such as trust, honesty, and commitment, are equally important online" (2001: 630). On SNS profiles and websites people may claim to like things they don't, or omit embarrassing true favorites, in order to create a public image in line with what they think others find attractive (Liu, Maes, & Davenport, 2006). On Last.fm, people routinely turn off the site's recording and display of their current listening when they are streaming artists inconsistent with the image they wish to project. They may also play cool artists on repeat when they are away in order to appear to like what they do not. Ellison, Heino, and Gibbs (2006) interviewed people who used a large online dating site. They found that people were generally truthful, but many exaggerated socially appealing qualities, claiming to weigh less than they really did, to be taller than they really were, or to be nonsmokers. They may have posted photos from when they were younger (Ellison et al., 2006). People building profiles in dating sites understood that they had to be credible and sought to manage the tension between that and the need to make themselves appear attractive enough to raise interest.

Sometimes being deceptive is more about presenting one's ideal self than a fictitious one. As one blogger (2birds1blog, 2008) wrote about choosing her SNS profile image:

> As a girl, I choose my facebook photo primarily by how unrealistically attractive I look in it. It's narcissistic, but you can't deny that you do the same thing. I'm not going to lie, sometimes when I'm getting ready to go out, I'll evaluate whether or not I'm lookin' "Facebook-worthy" that night. In other instances I'll even attend certain events just because I think I'll get a cute Facebook pic out of it. Overall, it's accepted that girls use their Facebook pic as an outlet to display their "Oh my Gawd I look HAWT!" pictures.

When people lied in dating sites, saying they were thin or a non-smoker, they sometimes genuinely believed that by the time they met the person they sought they would have lost weight or quit smoking (Ellison et al., 2006). What's more, people are sometimes limited in their self-knowledge and what they believe to be true about themselves may not be seen in them by others, a phenomenon Ellison et al. (2006) referred to as the "foggy mirror." Complicating the picture further, people may also lie because they have heard so much discourse about the dangers of meeting people online that they feel compelled to protect themselves by lying about who they are; hence, Whitty and Gavin's (2001) finding that women may lie about where they live, or my son's use of fake identities in his online activity. Teens and children are often taught by parents and other significant adults never to reveal their names, phone numbers, addresses, or any other identifying information online, essentially instructing them to lie.

Just as reduced cues and distance may encourage some to be more honest online by removing the social risk associated with telling the truth, technological design and affordances also influence deception. Ellison et al. (2006) found that one reason people lied about their ages in dating site profiles was to avoid being screened out in searches that clustered search results into systemically predetermined age ranges. Hancock, Thom-Santelli, and Ritchie (2004) had students keep a communication diary in which they recorded all of their efforts to mislead someone for seven days.

They found that, on average, people told 6.11 lies a day. Deception rates were highest on the telephone, followed by face to face communication. Email had the most honesty. They suggest this is because people realize they are less likely to get caught when using synchronous media that are neither stored nor replicable.

Authenticity and relationship

Regardless of how we present ourselves in digital environments, in most encounters others will have fairly limited cues with which to interpret us, and may or may not make of them the meanings we had intended. Social psychologists have described people as "cognitive misers" who try to get as much information as possible out of as few cues as we can. In mediated environments, where there are so many blanks to fill in, people make more out of others' small cues than we might face to face (Ellison et al., 2006). An ambiguous subject line, a single photograph, a short self-description, or a shared interest leads us to infer other information based on our stereotypes and assumptions about how social reality works. On Twitter, for example, someone took my frequent banter with one music business strategist to mean that I shared all of that person's positions. I don't.

We also "give off" as many cues as we "give" (Goffman, 1959), inadvertently revealing information about ourselves through the ways we behave rather than the content of our messages. Cues given off become highly informative in sparse cue situations (Ellison et al., 2006), so that, for example, poor spelling, which would never become relevant in most early face to face encounters, comes to be a highly significant marker of identity in textual media, taken to reveal sloppiness, lack of education, or other negative qualities. The dating site OkCupid (2009) conducted a lexical analysis of 500,000 first letters men wrote to women through the site in order to identify linguistic strategies that were more and less likely to lead to responses. They found that netspeak (e.g. "ur," "luv") was a turn-off, as were conventional openings such as "hi," "hey," and "hello." Letters beginning with "yo," "what's up," and "how's it going" were far more likely to get replies. Male self-effacement through terms such as "sorry," "apologize," and "awkward" generated more replies. As I wrote this paragraph I was "followed" by a new person on Twitter. His self-description said he could get me 16,000 Twitter followers in 90 days through an automated process. He had 4 followers. Even if I were out to collect as many followers as possible, I'd have had to go with the information given off over that given. We always form impressions that go beyond what others intended to present with the self-identifying cues provided. The point is that, in reduced cue environments, very small pieces of information, which were often not intended to be sources of information about the self, can become inordinately influential. This makes it considerably harder to present an inauthentic self.

Looking at the evidence, there's no compelling reason to assume that people who meet online are inherently less able or willing to represent themselves as they understand themselves to be than they are when they meet in unmediated contexts. People may lie online, but, then, face to face communication has never been a guarantor of truth, as people whose married lovers have sworn they were single or intended to leave their spouses will quickly tell you. The flip side of our fear of online deception is our gullibility in believing that vision prevents us from falling for lies.

As SIP argued, when people interact online with others over time, they become more likely to solicit and present "socially revealing, relational behavior" (Walther et al., 1994: 465), leading new acquaintances who pursue relationships to fairly accurate understandings of one another's identities. Over time, impressions formed through online interaction become increasingly similar to those formed face to face (Walther & Burgoon, 1992). When people meet online, they may need to make a leap of faith in deciding they know each other well enough to trust them (Henderson & Gilding, 2004). However, believing that you know and can trust someone else always requires a leap of faith, no matter how you meet.

Summary

When people meet online, it raises questions about whether they are honest about who they are, and, hence, whether they and the relationships they create can be trusted. At the core of the matter is the fact that contexts that transcend space and offer few social cues provide people with considerably more latitude and control in shaping the ways they present themselves to others. Different sites and technologies, with their differing affordances, influence self-presentation in different ways, whether that is by providing visible links to other people, privileging competence in web design over template use, or offering virtual attire and accoutrements to build identities.

However, as we've seen, the fact that the technological affordances of media do influence self-presentations does not mean that they determine them. Indeed, the same affordances can have opposite effects for different people in different circumstances. Some may feel free to lie, while others may feel free to be more honest than they would in person. Most people, in most cases, seem to err on the side of truthfulness, especially when they are linked to other people and social identities through their self-representations, although they may manipulate their self-presentations strategically and, at times, not entirely honestly. At this point, despite horror stories about online deception, there's no compelling reason to think that the people one meets online are inherently less trust-worthy than those we meet in embodied contexts. The identity foundations on which new relationships are built can be every bit as sturdy online as off.

6

Digital media in relational development and maintenance

I had been reading, teaching, and conducting research about online relationship formation for many years before I ever formed a close friendship online. Then I met and came to know Markus, a younger male Swedish graphic designer and musician whom I met through email. In late 2004, I spent a lot of time listening to two CDs by an obscure Swedish pop band. I sent them this email (which included my home address and a link to my university website) in appreciation:

Hello,

You are my reward for adolescent individuality. Here is why:

I went to high school in Urbana Illinois in the late 1970s/early 1980s. One of my friends was [*the person who owned the label on which the band's recordings had been released*]. I had multicolored hair and listened to the Kinks, the Buzzcocks, Sparks, and all kinds of other bands he'd never heard of. Everyone thought I was really weird. He didn't. We talked about music. A lot. I like to think I sparked what was until then his latent audiophile gene (I think he'd agree, although he overtook me within a very short time). He grew up to create [*their label*]. I grew up to have too little to do with all that music I still love.

And now, 20+ years later, he brings me you. Life can be so sweet.

Thanks for [*your record*]. It's making my winter so much more fun.

I'll be bopping around Northern Europe this summer, maybe you'll play some shows and I'll get to see you.

I hope you have a wonderful 2005.

The band member who happened to be their tech guy, Markus, wrote back quickly saying my email had made his day. A few days later, I wrote back. A week or so later, he wrote back. We began a correspondence that at times involved multiple emails every day for weeks, and rarely went more than two weeks between contacts. We exchanged more than 2,500 emails in four years.

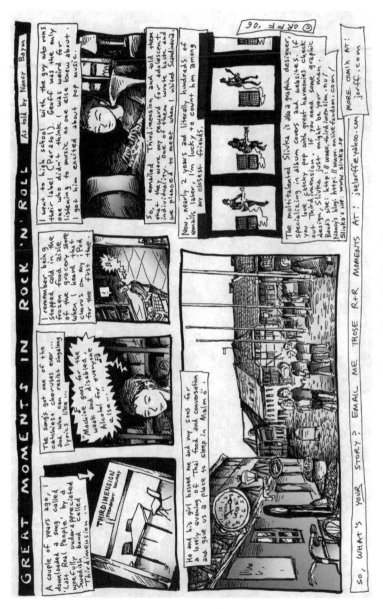

Cartoon 6.1: Joel Orff, 2006

We've vacationed together with our families. He loves that he gets to make an appearance in this chapter. Had we lived in the same town, we probably would have met. But, as we saw in the last chapter, our age and sex differences would likely have stood in the way of forming a close friendship, as would my lack of Swedish and his shyness with conversational English.

Markus and I illustrate how the internet has enabled fans and bands to become friends, a process that was integral to the growth of MySpace (boyd & Ellison, 2007) and which is seen on sites throughout the internet (Baym & Burnett, 2009). Our relationship and its development also demonstrate most of the patterns and issues seen in most relational development that begins online. The first part of this chapter continues last chapter's discussion of meeting online to examine how, when they do so at all, people like Markus and me, who meet via the internet, develop their relationships. We'll begin by addressing the early stages of relationships, the way communication changes as relationships develop and strengthen, and we'll look at the question of how relationships that begin online compare to those started face to face.

The second part of this chapter comes at the topic from the other side, asking how digital media fit into the landscape of interpersonal communication in personal relationships, regardless of how people first met. We'll see that people tend to add media as they grow closer and look specifically at the growing phenomenon of using social network sites (SNSs) in relational maintenance. In chapter 4, we asked whether internet use affected civic and political engagement. Here we'll address what effects the use of the internet has on people's social engagement. I'll also identify some of the main influences on which communication media people use when. The chapter closes by considering some of the ways relational media use remains an object of dispute, as different people and different groups develop different norms of appropriateness.

Building relationships with people we met online

Most relationships that start online do not become intimate, just as most people who meet face to face are unlikely to ever become more than distant acquaintances. Of the thousands of people with whom I have interacted online, some of whom I would call "friend," Markus is the only stranger who has made his way into my inner circle through the internet. Most have either drifted away completely or remained on the far peripheries of my social world. Others have become acquaintances.

Most interpersonal relationships are weak ties (Granovetter, 1973), limited in the range of activities, thoughts, and feelings partners exchange. The internet has expanded our access to weak ties and enabled us to have more specialized and intermittent contacts with more people. As we saw in chapter 4's discussion of social support in online communities and networks, among the important resources provided in weak tie relationships are feedback about ourselves, emotional support, information, advice, goods, and services. Weak ties are also those most likely to provide us with the bridging capital (Putnam, 2000) that those closest to us cannot, access to members of different social groups and the resources they can offer.

Like Markus and me, many, though by no means most, people have formed at least one enduring strong tie through digital media. Strong ties are those that encourage frequent, companionable contact. They are voluntary, mutually reciprocal, supportive of partners' needs, and they create long-term contact (Haythornthwaite, 2005). They provide bonding capital unavailable elsewhere. Resources exchanged in strong tie relationships run deep and may be emotionally and temporally expensive. As a result, we can't maintain too many strong tie relationships at any given time and have many fewer strong ties than weak ones.

However we meet, we form relationships by communicating with each other. Our messages are the tool with which we build and tinker with our connections, and the mirror through which we see them. Most relational communication is implicit. Unless there are problems, we rarely have detailed discussions about the correct label for our relationship, how close we think we are, and what obligations and responsibilities we believe our connection entails (Watzlawick, Beavin, & Jackson, 1967). For the most part, we show each other these things implicitly through the ways we communicate with each other. As we move from strangers to relational partners, we communicate more often, and our communication takes on consistent patterns. Once a relationship is established, every interaction we have serves as an opportunity to reaffirm it by behaving just as we always do, to end it by saying something that cannot be repaired, or to negotiate it by communicating a little differently from our norm.

Early idealization

When people meet one another online, especially in media with few identifying cues, they often seem to like one another more than they would if they had met in person. This phenomenon of "hyperpersonal communication" (Walther, 1996) was first documented in experiments comparing groups of students who worked on projects together in person or remotely via text-based online discussion. It has since been affirmed in naturalistic studies (e.g. Henderson & Gilding, 2004; McKenna et al., 2002). I had taught this concept for years, but was still taken aback as I watched it happen to me with Markus. Even knowing the reasons (which I'll cover just below) that I might be driven to find him unrealistically attractive, I still found myself knowingly exaggerating his appeal. My husband, appropriately confident of my affections, even took to jokingly referring to him as my "Swedish boyfriend."

Walther proposed three reasons we might like the people we meet online more than those we meet offline, at least early on. In online impression formation, sparse cues leave a great deal of room for imagining the other. When, as they often do, online relationships form because of shared interests, it is easy to imagine other shared qualities not yet discussed. When we decide that the other has appeals such as humor, good response time, or writing style (Baker, 2008), it is easy to fill in the blanks about their other traits with ideals. Markus's facility with words, cleverness, and status as a member of a band I really liked led me to assume much more about him than those qualities could reveal. Although some of those early assumptions were right, others were not. It turned out, for instance, that, although we have overlapping musical taste, our taste is more different than similar. Walther also argued that we might appear more attractive to others in online meetings because sparse cues give us more control over our messages, letting us be more selective in what we reveal and when. My first email to Markus, as you can see above, was extremely selective in which pieces of my autobiography I chose to foreground (my music-oriented high school self, my approximate age, and travel plans that could result in our meeting). Third, Walther suggested that hyperpersonal communication could occur because the reduced-cue environment allows people to focus more on message production. This might lead to their creating better messages, presenting a self online that really is more attractive than that same person could be under the demands and distractions of body to body interaction. Asynchronous media, in particular, allow people to revise. I certainly reread and rewrote many of the emails I sent Markus when we were first getting to know each other.

A reason for hyperpersonal communication that Walther does not discuss is hinted at in Ellen Ullman's (1997) tale of meeting a new man online. She and he exchanged emails filled with literary passages and dreams. But when they finally met, they realized they could only "speak in emails." In retrospect, she saw that part of the attraction had been the anticipation of hearing from him and, ultimately, of meeting. The very title of the film *You've Got Mail* speaks to the excitement of anticipation in online relationships. In the first months of our friendship, getting a message from Markus was a guaranteed extra happy moment, and the anticipation of and pleasure in his notes' arrival retains an appeal unique among my friendships.

Relational development

As once-weak ties develop and strengthen, communication patterns change to reflect and build the evolving relationship. Parks and Floyd (1996) developed a scale to measure relational development (later modified by Chan & Cheng, 2004), which my colleague Andrew Ledbetter and I found helpful in studying relational strength in Last.fm friendships (Baym & Ledbetter, 2009).

One way in which communication changes as people get closer is that our discussions span a wider range of topics, which we address at greater depth. We also become increasingly direct about our feelings, and come to trust each other with our personal confidences. From the start, Markus and I disclosed about our past, our attitudes, music, where we lived, and how we spent our days. Over time, we had broadened the topic range so much that, when we met in person six months after the first emails, he was surprised that I did not know his parents' careers.

Self-disclosure is one of the most powerful communication practices we have for building a relationship, although it can backfire if one shares too much too soon or shares something the other person finds unappealing. Relationship theorists have described relationship formation as a process of "social penetration" in which people grow closer by revealing ever deeper aspects of themselves, peeling back the layers of an onion until they knew one another to the core and have attained intimacy (Altman & Taylor, 1973). This approach has been critiqued for envisioning the self as a static entity with multiple layers rather than the ever-shifting dynamic and flexible set of constructions depicted in the last chapter, but it remains the case that we can't get to know one another well and build trust without self-disclosure. There is nothing about a low-cue medium that makes self-disclosure impossible. To the contrary, as chapter 5 showed, it may even make it easier. The pace at which we disclose may be different online from off, but it is otherwise akin to the process face to face (Walther, 1994).

As relationships strengthen, we also become more interdependent, influencing one another's behaviors, thoughts, and feelings, which is reflected in and enacted through communication. We become better able to predict the other. We come to know one another's communication styles, so that we can read between the lines of one another's messages. We may use secret terms or words and phrases with private connotations or give one another nicknames. Markus and I, for instance, fell into the habit of beginning our emails with an ever-changing array of silly affectionate greetings (e.g., Hello handsome, Hola guapa). We introduce our partners to other friends and our families, and we are willing to expend effort to ensure that the relationship endures (Parks, 2006; Parks & Floyd, 1996).

At the start of the last chapter, we saw Tom and his eventual wife go from internet to telephone to dinner at the same table in a day. It is not always this fast, but as relationships that begin online develop, they tend to add other media in a predictable pattern. We'll return to this phenomenon of "media multiplexity" (Haythornthwaite, 2005) below. Often beginning in public discussion, online partners add private one-on-one interaction via messaging, email, or chat. Without giving up those means of communication, they begin to include the telephone. Once they've spoken on the phone, odds that a pair will meet in person increase (McKenna et al., 2002). Of the pairs McKenna et al. (2002) studied, 62 percent had spoken to someone they met online on the phone, 56 percent had exchanged pictures, 54 percent had written a snail-mail letter, and 54 percent had met face to face. In our survey of friends on Last.fm, 47 percent said they had never met. Of those, most were interested in meeting: 60 percent said they would meet if it were convenient, 13 percent were split between being willing to make plans to meet and already having made such plans. However, 27 percent of respondents said they were not interested in meeting their Last.fm friend. The more personalized and diverse our use of communication media becomes, the more we relinquish control over our interactions, giving the other multiple access points to our lives, and extending our potential interdependence.

Markus and I share a fondness for the written word, and went from email to snail mail. Six weeks after we first met, he sent me a hard-to-find single with an otherwise unreleased song I'd asked him for. With it he included a letter (as well as a few other treats like buttons and stickers). Though I doubt he thought it through, his letter, the first handwritten tangible marker of our relationship, contained his first deep disclosures. In it he shared his sadness at the recent unexpected loss of his girlfriend's father (a disclosure which also served to show me the depth of his connection to her) and his fears of his parents' and his own mortality. A few months later, when my travels took me to Northern Europe, we used email to plan our meeting. When I got to Europe, Markus and I began text messaging on our mobile phones (the text message he sent me was, embarrassingly, the first one I'd ever received – I had to read the manual and fumble my way through a typo-ridden response). Not until the day we met did we talk on the telephone. How was our first meeting? Awkward. There were long silences. Markus felt nervous and lost confidence in his English. But I met (and was smitten by) his girlfriend, he met my sons and carried the little one around town on his shoulders, and the reservoir of knowledge and affection we had built carried us through. In the time since, I've visited them in Sweden, they've visited me and my father in Copenhagen, and they and their baby daughter have come to stay with us in the United States. Writing remains our primary mode of interaction, but being together now feels easy and familiar.

Comparing online to offline relationships

As we develop relationships that begin online, we increasingly add media that allow us to use a wider range of social cues. Accordingly, limits on those relationships that can be attributed to sparse cues become increasingly irrelevant. That has not stopped people from trying to compare "online" to "offline" relationships. Some studies have found friendships that develop face to face to be slightly more developed (Chan & Cheng, 2004; Mesch & Talmud, 2006; Parks & Roberts, 1998), with partners who met online spending less time together, engaging in fewer shared activities, and, in some studies (e.g. Mesch & Talmud, 2006) but not others (Parks & Roberts, 1998), engaging in less discussion of personal problems and romantic relationships. The one important exception seems to be that cross-sex friendships that began online (like mine and Markus's) may be of higher quality than same-sex friendships, in contrast to those relationships that began offline (Chan & Cheng, 2004).

One reason online friendships might appear less developed is that they are newer (Mesch & Talmud, 2006), and hence have not yet had the chance to develop. Longitudinal studies that follow online friendships over time do not show meaningful differences between them and offline friendships. Chan and Cheng (2004) found that the differences between online and offline friendships increased within the first year but then diminished, and the relationships converged over time. They speculate that online friendships are more tentative in early stages, but after six months to a year grow quickly and become more like offline friendships (Chan & Cheng, 2004). McKenna et al. (2002) also tracked friendship pairs over time and found that online relationships lasted well over two years, comparing favorably with offline relationships. After two years, 71 percent of romantic relationships and 75 percent of all relationships begun online were still going. Most had grown closer and stronger.

In the end, then, people can and do develop meaningful personal relationships online. Many of them remain weak and specialized, used to exchange resources around a fairly narrow set of topics of shared interest. These relationships make important contributions to people's lives, especially when they allow people to interact about interests and concerns that their close relational partners do not share. Pairs who do become closer interact through multiple media, eventually making the influence of the internet difficult to conceptually distinguish from the many other influences on their partnership. Reduced cues may be an issue in early stages of relationships, or in those that never have any prospect of going beyond initial encounters, but over time people can reveal themselves to one another verbally and nonverbally until they form understandings of one another as rich as, or richer than, those they hold of people they meet in any other way. I suspect I know more about Markus, and knew some of it earlier, than most of the people he communicates with primarily through talk. I know he knows me better than many of my local friends.

Mediated relational maintenance

Multiplexity

I've been using the internet daily for almost twenty years. I participate in many online environments where I interact with strangers. I have made hundreds if not thousands of acquaintances, but I've only invited one to share a family vacation. In contrast, I have used the internet to communicate with all of my close friends and family as well as hundreds of other people I first met in person in my neighborhood, work, and travels. This is normal. The public's fascination with new relationship formation online obscures the important, if mundane, fact that, like the telephone, the internet's primary use as a relational medium for most people is to communicate with people they also know face to face. "Online" relationships turn into "offline" ones much less often than "offline" friendships turn into "online" ones. The former shouldn't hog the debate. The rise of SNSs, which are used primarily to replicate connections that exist offline rather than to build new ones (boyd & Ellison, 2007), has cast this phenomenon into the spotlight, but taking offline ties online is a practice as old as the internet. An American random-sample telephone survey in the late 1990s, for instance, found that 41 percent of the reasons offered for home use of the internet had to do with supporting and maintaining meaningful relationships (Stafford, Kline, & Dimmick, 1999). In this section, we'll look at how media are used in pre-existing personal relationships, surveying the factors that influence our decisions to use some media rather than others in some circumstances and relationships. Most relationships are characterized by "media multiplexity," meaning that they are conducted through more than one medium, and that closer relationships use more media (Haythornthwaite, 2005).

In one of my studies of media use in college student relationships, 496 college students assessed the extent to which they used the internet in their social circles (Baym, Zhang, & Lin, 2004). The majority of their interpersonal internet communication was within pairs who also spoke on the telephone or face to face. We also asked them to estimate what percentage of total interaction in a specific relationship was conducted through each medium and found that this had no bearing on how close or satisfying they perceived that relationship to be (Baym, Zhang, Kunkel, Lin, & Ledbetter, 2007). They were also asked to report on their most recent significant voluntary social interaction online, face to face, or on the telephone (Baym et al., 2004). Despite their tendency to rank media in the order that we saw in the opening quotations in chapter 3, across random interactions, the statistical differences in quality amongst media were few and slight. The telephone was perceived as equal in quality to face to face conversation. Online interaction (primarily email) was perceived as slightly lower quality, but the difference was very small – a quarter of a point on a five-point scale – and a very small percentage of total variation in quality was accounted for by medium. By far the most influential predictor of the quality of an interaction turned out to be the relationship type. People in close relationships had high-quality interactions regardless of the medium through which they interacted.

In a related study, 51 students kept a diary of all their voluntary social interactions for several days (Baym et al., 2004). Only 1 of the 51 reported having only face to face interactions or internet interactions during the reported days. In contrast, 32 people (64 percent) reported conducting interactions face to face, on the phone, and online; 13 people reported no significant internet interactions; 6 people reported no significant telephone calls; 2 did not report any face to face conversations. There were nearly as many internet interactions as there were telephone interactions, but most interactions were face to face. This is in keeping with previous studies finding that the internet is used on a par with the telephone in personal relationships (Dimmick, Kline, & Stafford, 2000; Flanagin & Metzger, 2001; Stafford et al., 1999).

I came at this from a different angle in a later study, starting with friendship pairs on Last.fm and asking what other media they used (Baym & Ledbetter, 2009). One of our goals was to explore the diversity of ways people engage one another online as well as offline. Although almost a third said Last.fm was the only way they communicated in this relationship, on average the pairs reported using between two and three other ways of interacting with each other. In addition to being friends on Last.fm, many of the pairs also used Instant Messaging (42 percent), other websites (34.7 percent), and email (31.3 percent). A third of the pairs said they also communicated face to face. Of those who had ever met face to face, 60 percent said they saw one another "regularly" or "all the time"; 23.6 percent used the telephone and 21.3 percent texted; 1 pair in 20 even used the postal service.

Maintaining relationships through SNSs

Since 2008, SNSs have become mainstream sites of relational maintenance for those who already know one another. Lenhart and Madden (2007) found that 91 percent of US teens who use SNSs report that they do so in order to connect with friends. Mayer and Puller (2007) pulled data from Facebook users at Texas A&M to see how they met and found that, of those who gave a reason, 26 percent met through a school organization, 16 percent through another friend, 14 percent had attended the same high school, and 12 percent had taken a course together. Only 0.4 percent met online. Relationship maintenance, rather than relational creation, has also been found to be a primary motive for using Cyworld (Choi, 2006) and MySpace (boyd, 2006). Though people were far less likely to already know one another on Last.fm than were pairs in these studies, Baym and Ledbetter (2009) still found that over half (52.9 percent) knew each other before becoming Last.fm friends.

Although people in close relationships do use SNSs with each other, most relationships maintained via SNSs are weak. Baron (2008) found that students reported an average of 72 "real" friends in their 229 Facebook friends, a 1:3 ratio almost identical to Ellison, Steinfeld, and Lampe's (2009) result. Ledbetter and I (Baym & Ledbetter, 2009) found that, while a few people reported close relationships on Last.fm, on average Last.fm friends rated their relationships just below the midpoint on measures of relational development. The range of relationship types included amongst Last.fm friends included everything from strangers who had since decided they didn't like one another to lifelong best-friends, family members, and romantic partners.

SNSs allow people to exchange messages directly with one another, through asynchronous messages and real-time chat, but the vast majority of friendship pairs do not seem to ever do this. In their analysis of 362 million messages on Facebook, Golder et al. (2007) found that only 15.1 percent of friends ever exchanged messages. Baron (2008) found that 60 percent of Facebook users wrote on others' walls either never or less than once a week.

In their analysis of over 200,000 MySpace messages, Gilbert, Karahalios and Sandvig (2008) found that 43.5 percent of friends never commented on one another's profiles, and only 4 percent ever exchanged ten or more comments. As we saw above, however, scant direct SNS communication does not imply little relational communication since pairs are likely to be communicating through other media (Baym & Ledbetter, 2009; Haythornthwaite, 2005).

Those who do communicate through these sites are accomplishing many aims. For the most part, they are probably keeping one another posted. Some may interact in order to convert weak ties into strong ones (Donath & boyd, 2004; Ellison et al., 2007). but they may also be engaged in microcoordination, as they use the sites to organize joint activities on the fly (Humphreys, 2007; Ling, 2004). This is especially so when these sites are well integrated with mobile devices. As we saw in the last chapter, there is also evidence that in some cases SNSs allow exchanges more emotionally risky than people would brave face to face. Larsen's (2007) work on Arto.dk shows that participants, in particular adolescent girls, often leave emotionally effusive messages proclaiming their love and admiration for one another on each other's profiles, a form of communication out of keeping with Danish norms. Kim and Yun's (2007) research likewise suggests that for Koreans, who may avoid negative emotional communication face to face, Cyworld can offer a venue for such communication, with one informant reporting that she had "been able to save many relationships thanks to my minihompy [profile]" (Kim & Yun, 2007).

The success of Facebook and other SNSs as relationship maintenance tools comes from their wide but selective reach: people can communicate with multiple weak ties simultaneously. Messages can be delivered to all friends via status updates, for instance, or select friends through wall posts. Equally, if not more importantly, people can share photographs. As of this writing, Facebook is the world's largest photo-sharing site, hosting over 1 billion photos. Even without direct interaction, simply having access to one another's updates on an SNS may facilitate a sense of connection (e.g. Humphreys, 2007). Several of the friends who took our Last.fm survey mentioned the sense of connection they maintained with the other as one of the benefits they received from maintaining a relationship on the site. Baron (2008: 85) cites a respondent who describes it as "a way of maintaining a friendship without having to make any effort whatsoever." Different SNSs offer different packages of affordances, Last.fm emphasizes music, while Facebook emphasizes people, and other sites emphasize many other things. When people use SNSs to connect with strong ties, it provides another range of options for exchanging bonding resources, such as affection, advice, and support. When people connect with weak ties through SNSs, it increases their access to bridging capital and expands the range of resources on which they can draw. Intense SNS use can enhance bridging social capital, giving people access to more resources of different types than they would likely have otherwise (Ellison et al., 2007).

Influences on media use in relationships

What determines which media people choose in a relationship? One factor is how sociable a person is. Highly sociable people may communicate via any medium they can. A study of Japanese youth found that those with more social skills used more mobile voice and PC email and less mobile texting (Ishii, 2006). People with social anxiety may prefer media with fewer cues (McKenna et al., 2002). Relational media use is also shaped by the demands of cultural contexts and peer groups. The Finns, sometimes described as "silent in two languages" (Puro, 2002: 19), may be particularly appreciative of the mobile phone, as seen in the leadership and success of Nokia in that industry and in the daily practice of the Finns, where mobile phone use is as high as it is anywhere in the world. Puro (2002) argues that the mobile phone forces Finns to be sociable despite a culture that eschews small talk and speaking without a reason, values the succinct delivery of information, and appreciates silence. Baron and Hård af Segerstad (in press) compared mobile phone use in Sweden, the United States, and Japan and found that some of the differences in public media use could be explained by cultural norms. In Japan, for example, where there is an expectation of public quiet in places such as subways and sidewalks, text messaging is used far more often than in the other two countries.

Finnish teenagers have highly ritualized ways of using mobile phones that demonstrate how different media use can be in different peer groups (Kasesniemi & Rautiainen, 2002). Text messaging is pervasive amongst teens where it serves to solidify their peer culture. In addition to continuous coordination, they also share risqué jokes, which they keep secret from their parents. Although these text messages, or SMSs, are ephemeral, these teenagers collect them, writing them down in notebooks, some of which are specially designed and marketed for this purpose. Text messages are not just direct means of communication, they are objects to be compared, traded, and composed with friends.

Media use and its meanings are also shaped by the stage of a relationship within its cultural context. In dating relationships amongst young people in Israel in the early 2000s, for instance (Hijazi-Omari & Ribak, 2008), young men presented mobile phones to young women as a sign of their relational commitment. The telephones, which, like the romances themselves, had to be kept secret from the women's parents, required networks of friends to safeguard them, which also shaped preferences for what telephones should look like (small and unremarkable in appearance). A tether to the man on the one hand and a resistance of the parents on the other, the phone freed young women from their fathers and mothers (although the maneuvers required to keep it secret from them continued to demonstrate parental authority) but situated them under greater control by their boyfriends. Traditions such as these may be short-lived, however, as, within a few short years, Palestinian norms around mobile phones had changed such that parents were buying mobile phones for their teenage daughters. Sarch's (1993) study of telephone use in dating relationships also showed how the use of one medium rather than another can be mobilized in the early stages of romantic relationships. Interviews with women revealed how telephone calls were used to negotiate intimacy. A relationship could be measured in terms of how often the two spoke on the phone, for how long, and, perhaps most importantly, whether the calls resulted in plans to see one another. As these two examples show, relational media use can be, in part, a way to symbolize and enact our gender roles as men and women (Hijazi-Omari & Ribak, 2008; Ling, 2004; Sarch, 1993).

People seem more likely to use the internet to communicate with friends than family, further demonstrating the influence of relationship type on media use. In a large international survey, Chen et al. (2002) found that email was used more with friends than with relatives. Quan-Haase, Wellman, Witte, and Hampton (2002), using the same data, found that email and face to face conversation were equally frequent amongst nearby friends, each constituting 29 percent of all contact. Email was less frequent with local family, however, making up just 17 percent of all contact compared to the 27 percent of family interactions conducted face to face. Relational intimacy is also important. The more intimate the American college students' relationships I studied, the more likely they were to use face to face conversations and telephone calls. Their internet use neither increased nor decreased with relational closeness. On the other hand, Last.fm friends' responses to open-ended questions asking why they befriended one another revealed that, for many of them, part of a close relationship was bringing the other person along to any medium they discovered.

How far from one another people live is also an important influence on which media we use. Locally, face to face and telephone calls seem to predominate. Chen et al. (2002) and Quan-Haase et al. (2002) found that, internationally, the telephone was the medium most used in local relationships. Amongst college students, local relationships were most likely to use face to face conversation, followed by the telephone (Baym et al., 2004), a difference which can likely be attributed to the differences between living on a residential campus and the kinds of lifestyles more likely encompassed by these other scholars' international online sample. Local interactions do use the internet, however, as we saw in chapter 4's discussion of neighborhood and civic digital engagement. Our students reported using the internet in just over a third of all local relationships (Baym et al., 2004). The affordances of the mobile telephone – it is small, portable, and can be used relatively quickly and discreetly in a wide variety of circumstances – enhance its usefulness in local relationships. Brief calls between people who see one another regularly can activate emotional bonds, enacting and reinforcing closeness (Licoppe & Heurtin, 2002). Mobile communication devices also allow people to microcoordinate their actions, for example calling to ask whether to stop and buy milk on the way home, suggesting a spur-of-the-moment get-together, or telling someone you're running late (Ling, 2004; Ling & Yttri, 2002). Mobile phones are also widely used for security, so that, should something untoward happen, people will be able to reach emergency responders as well as friends and family. For teens, who as we have seen may be particularly enmeshed in mobile phone networks with their peers, this microcoordination can become hypercoordination, such that they may feel left out of their social circles if deprived of their mobile phones for even a short time (Ling & Yttri, 2002), a feeling I've seen displayed by many adults as well. The continuous relational accessibility enabled by mobile phones thus keeps local peers and family more tightly interdependent, but can also come to feel overwhelming and imprisoning for that very reason.

In long-distance relationships, the telephone does not seem to have the same functionality. Survey studies in the early 2000s found that email was the predominant means of keeping in touch across long-distance time-zone differences (Dimmick et al., 2000). In distant relationships, Quan-Haase et al. (2002) found that 49 percent of all social contact with kin was conducted online, while 62 percent of interactions with friends used the internet. Dimmick et al.'s (2000) research revealed that email was considered superior to the telephone for such communication; nearly half reported using the long-distance telephone less now that they were online. Our students' internet interactions were more likely to be long-distance than local, and their long-distance interactions were more likely to be online than on the telephone (Baym et al., 2004).

These findings about the preference for internet over telephone may be in part an artifact of the pricing structures surrounding mobile phone calls in the early 2000s. In the USA at that time, text messaging was an expensive add-on which greatly limited its use. It's possible that with the incorporation of messaging into

American phone plans, we would see more telephone use in long-distance relationships now. On the other hand, that was already true for many of the respondents in Chen et al. and Quan-Haase et al.'s studies. Given the association of the telephone with intimacy (Baym et al., 2007), it makes sense that the internet and telephones serve different niches in long-distance communication (Dimmick et al., 2000). The telephone may best serve close relationships across distance, while the internet, with its broad reach and asynchronous possibilities, may best serve weaker long-distance ties.

Effects of internet use on other relationships

We've seen that meaningful relationships can be established through mediation and that mediation can be used successfully in existing relationships, but that leaves open the question of what engagement with the internet and other communication technology use do to our relationships with other people – one of the core issues we saw raised in the public discourse in chapter 2. Do new communication technologies undermine or replace face to face relationships? Just as critics cautioned that digital communities would replace locally grounded communities, the internet and mobile media raise fears that digital media lead us to substitute shallow empty relationships for authentic personal connections. Instead of being present with those who share our physical environments, we may become separated, isolated, and never more than partially anywhere.

For example, some studies have found that internet users spend less time with family and friends. Katz and Rice (2002) found that people who had used the internet recently were more likely to have been away from their homes, and Cole (2000) found that, compared to non-users, internet users socialized slightly less with household members. Nie, Hillygus, and Erbring (2002) found that internet users spent less in-person and telephone time with friends and family. They quantified this, saying that each minute online takes away 20 seconds with family members, 7 seconds with friends, 11 seconds with colleagues, and adds 45 seconds of time spent alone. However, in Cole's study, 92 percent of the internet users report that they were spending the same amount of time or more time with family since going online, raising the possibility that internet users are more likely to have careers or other reasons for being home less often and that, if the correlation is real, the internet is not its cause.

The introduction of communication technology into relational life has problems, and we'll turn to them soon, but making us less communicative with others does not seem to be one of them. My work with college students (Baym et al., 2004) and Last.fm (Baym & Ledbetter, 2009) showed that media use and face to face communication were positively correlated. The more students reported using the internet to maintain their social relationships, the more likely they were to use face to face conversations, telephone calls, and mail. Last.fm friends' use of any one medium positively predicted use of all the others, with especially strong associations between face to face interaction and telephone calls, texting and telephone calls, telephone calls and IM, and texting and IM. Others have found this too. A diary study by Copher, Kanfer, and Walker (2002) had American community leaders keep records of all interactions that went beyond a greeting for one week. When they compared heavy to light email users, they found that heavy email users also used proportionately more face to face communication for personal interactions than light users. Heavy emailers also had "greater numbers and percentages of communications, time spent communicating, and [communication partners] than light email users" across media (Copher et al., 2002: 274).

Random-sample surveys of Americans have also found that internet users keep in touch with more people, including family, friends, and professional colleagues, than do non-users (Cole, 2000; Rainie et al., 2000), although, in Cole's study, users reported about the same number of friends outside their household (an average of 11.5) as did non-users. In a study that looked directly at whether meeting new people online substitutes for social ties that are lacking offline, Matei and Ball-Rokeach (2002) compared internet users in diverse neighborhoods in Los Angeles. They found that people who had more social ties in their local communities were more likely to use the internet in order to meet new people. They concluded that "belongers belong everywhere." In the Japanese context, Ishii (2006) found that the youth who used more email widened their social circles to include more distant friends.

Studies that look at all internet use, rather than just relational internet use, also show that internet users are generally more social than non-users. In a 2000 poll, the Pew Internet and American Life Project found that 72 percent of internet users, including long-time and heavy users, reported having visited with family or friends 'yesterday' while only 61 percent of non-users did. Katz and Rice (2002) found that people who had used the internet the longest were most likely to have met with four to five friends in the prior week, while those who had not heard of the internet (who, you will recall from chapter 4, were most likely to know their neighbors) were least likely to have met with friends. Robinson, Kestnbaum, Neustadtl, and Alvarez (2002) conducted a random-sample survey of the American population and walked them through the last 24 hours of their lives in 15 minute increments. Internet users reported spending three times as long attending social events and reported significantly more conversation than non-users. Internet users also slept less, spent less time on personal hygiene, and had more free time, giving some indications of what might really be displaced by time spent online.

People also use the internet together. Cole (2000) found that 47 percent of internet users report spending some time each week using the internet with family members. An observational study of children's computer use at home (Orleans & Laney, 2000) found that the internet provides many opportunities for children to interact. Online materials served as a topic for conversation, children searched online for commonly valued items together, they found opportunities for social experimentation together, and the internet allowed them to demonstrate esteemed knowledge and skills (Orleans & Laney, 2000). Though I must admit that in my own home there are times when familial computer use has detracted from family together time, I also value the hours of brotherly bonding my sons have spent side by side – sometimes in the same chair – in front of the screen playing a game or showing one another their coolest new find.

Uncertain norms

The presence of communication technologies during face to face encounters can be problematic, though, and people are deeply divided as to how and whether these technologies can be incorporated into body to body conversation without becoming intrusions. Work on the mobile phone, especially Lee Humphreys' (2005), shows the nuance with which we reorganize our interactions when someone makes or takes a call during a face to face conversation. Using Goffman's (1963, 1971) terms, she describes phone calls as making "withs" into "singles" and shows how people singled by telephone calls accommodate the situation by looking elsewhere, engaging in other activities, walking ahead, or listening in.

As technologies are domesticated, they move from being completely novel to routine. For this to happen, as I argued in chapter 2, people have to get beyond the utopian and dystopian reactions to wrestle with messy nuances. This book has shown that many of those nuances are shaking out into order already. Others, like the question of when it's appropriate to take or make a mobile phone call, are far from resolved. In closing this chapter, we'll look at three sets of issues around digital communication technologies that show that we are still in a process of making sense of these media and their meanings in our relational lives. First, I'll address disagreements over the local and negatively emotional use of online communication. I'll turn then to the question of what a "friend" is when three-quarters of SNS friends aren't "real." Finally, we'll look at the question of how much information is too much.

When is it appropriate?

To say that the internet is used locally is not to say that everyone thinks it always should be or agrees on how it should be. A few years ago I conducted focus-group interviews with college students to explore their sentiments about using the internet in their local personal relationships (Baym, 2005). Though my university is not noted for the diversity of the student body, these students' attitudes ranged widely, showing just how unsettled and potentially relationally problematic the topic could be. Several of the students had integrated the internet into their local relational lives as a way to build relationships and to keep them going. One student told me: "I think with people that I don't know, like I've met people and we've just hung out once or twice, and then we get online and just become all of a sudden much closer." Another reported using email as a way of extending last night's party through the following day:

> If my friends and I all went out the night before and something happened like I fell down the stairs or something we would send an email about like "is anyone falling down the stairs?" just like real quick one-liners and they'll go out to like all 20 of us, you know. Just like simple little things that keep the joke running, that keep our days kinda like goin' through. And that's why I'm always like checkin' my email to see if anyone's like updated the joke or comeback.

People also said they used email to plug the gaps in the time they couldn't spend with their closest friends:

> I have long-time friends from home that go here too and so we email back and forth. Cuz they live [here], but they're also from home too, so there's more of a connection. So I email them like basically my whole week . . . We just kinda keep our email up even though we can't really talk everyday . . . even though we're really busy, and even though we're so close, like physically location, but we still can be together every single day.

However, other students saw the local use of the internet quite differently. As one student I interviewed put it, "I have [used email locally] a couple of times, which is weird. I'll be like 'ok well I'll come get you' and you're not talking to 'em. And that's just weird." Another woman I interviewed seemed to find the idea of communicating with local people online rather than in person almost offensive:

> I live in a [dorm] and I have my friend who lives on the third floor and I live on the second floor and instead of walking down the steps to talk to me she thinks it's cute to IM me. And I'm just like "hang on," and I just walk up there and I talk to her . . . I wouldn't email [a friend] if she lived you know like down the street. I can get in my car and just go see her or leave a message "call me back I have to talk to you."

The students also disagreed about whether it was appropriate to end a romantic relationship online or to use the internet as a means of confronting friends who had offended you when you were last together. Some loved the internet for ending relationships – especially women – while others were horrified at the thought. Most thought it was not a good way to handle conflict, but others explained that, since they anger easily, they would understand why their friend had chosen that medium, or that they were glad their friend had a means of raising an issue they didn't feel able to confront in person. At least one indicated that, were she confronted via the internet, she would consider it a sign of such disrespect that it would be grounds for ending the friendship.

What's a "friend"?

Another area in which we see disagreement is the practice of "friending" in SNSs. Donath (2007) posits that SNSs "may transform the concepts of friendship, personal acquaintance, and public celebrity," a possibility she connects to "related cultural reconfigurations, from the reduced autonomy of American youth to the increased attention to the private lives of public figures." When friends in an SNS can be strangers, admirers, confidants, co-workers, family, and a host of other relationship types, yet all be called the same thing on the site, it triggers inevitable confusion. If "friend" in an SNS doesn't mean what it means offline, or rather, if people one would introduce or consider as a "real" friend offline are only a subset of the people under that umbrella on a SNS, then there is potential for conflict over what it means to be a "friend" and who does and doesn't get included.

Many scholars of friendship have noted the ambiguity of personal connections (e.g. Parks, 2006; Rawlins, 1992). Online, as well as off, "the very term 'friendship' is both vague and symbolically charged and may denote many different types of relationship" (Kendall, 2002: 141). Partners within the same relationship may differ in how they categorize it. In SNSs, however, the technical necessity of labeling connections enhances this ambiguity. Pairs may differ on what kind of relationship their "friendship" represents

(Fono & Raynes-Goldie, 2006); people may be held to account for the behaviors of "friends" they barely know (boyd & Heer, 2006; Donath & boyd, 2004); people may not be sure or disagree about what obligations such links entail (Kim & Yun, 2007). Ambiguity can lead to conflict. Speaking of the term "friend" in LiveJournal, Fono and Raynes-Goldie (2006) say its "reflexivity and multiplicity of meaning causes much of the social anxiety, conflict and misunderstanding." In Cyworld, where the Korean kinship term "ilchon" is used, similar problems arise. "The ilchon metaphor," wrote Kim and Yum (2007), "created varying levels of relational tensions, depending on the degree of intimacy that the word ilchon connoted to users." When there are variants of labels available, that too can cause problems. One of boyd's (2006) teenage interviewees described MySpace's "Top 8" feature that allowed people to list eight of their friends above all the others as "psychological warfare."

How much information?

The 2008 word of the year, as decided by the editors of Webster's *World Dictionary*, was "overshare," meaning too much self-disclosure. In a video posted to YouTube about this, the chief editor explains they chose it not just because it functions as both noun and verb, but because it reflected an important trend in public communication. "Some people use it disparagingly, they don't like oversharing," he explained, "Other people think oversharing is good. And sometimes there's a generational shift in how people look at this practice and therefore view the world." The cultural turmoil regarding how much disclosure is appropriate to whom under what circumstances, and its flip side, how much privacy must be protected, is indeed intense. Many online forums now use the acronym "TMI" for "Too Much Information," indicating both how routinized "over"-disclosure has become and how uncertain its appropriateness remains.

One element of the urge to disclose is, as we have discussed many times, the limits on cues, which can make it easier to be honest and make negative social repercussions of such honesty seem more distant and less likely. Another is the problem of collapsed contexts (boyd & Heer, 2006). When we are disclosing to one person or group on an SNS, list, or community, our behavior is also visible to many other people. We may have known they could see it, yet not considered them part of its audience. One man I know took to ignoring Facebook status updates because he got so turned off by new parent friends' posts about their children's body excretions, messages that grandparents and other new parents might care about (though perhaps such news is TMI even for them). When we post pictures of ourselves on holiday and relaxing with friends, or whine about our work, it may not be oversharing, but may still not be entirely appropriate for the professional acquaintances and colleagues in our circles who may nonetheless see it.

The public mobile phone conversation is another example of a new communication practice that has unsettled the norms about disclosure. Many who object to having to overhear half of a telephone call seem particularly incensed when that call is personal. We've all heard disclosures we really didn't want to when listening to other people's unavoidable phone conversations. Most of the time the speakers seem not to care that they are being overheard, expecting, as Goffman (1971) put it, that unintended audiences will provide "civil inattention" by pretending not to notice.

Other times, people may just not be aware of who their audience is. People on SNSs, blogs, or discussion forums may not realize all possible readers of their messages. In Facebook, for instance, most people reveal personal data on their profiles, but rarely adjust their privacy settings to control others' access to that information (Gross & Acquisti, 2005), meaning, in Facebook's case, that everyone in their entire university or regional network could see their profiles. University students are sometimes shocked to realize their professors and potential employers can see their profiles. I was taken aback when I first realized that when I wrote on a friend's Facebook wall, that message was broadcast to all of our mutual friends in their newsfeeds. When personal information about us is accessed by unexpected viewers, the results can be embarrassing or life-altering. Information posted in SNSs has resulted in lost jobs, revoked visas, imprisonment, and tarnished reputations (Snyder, Carpenter, & Slauson, 2006).

Summary

The questions around relationships and new media cannot be answered with utopian or dystopian oversimplifications, nor can they be understood as direct consequences either of technology or of the people who use it. Technological affordances intersect with personal, social, and cultural influences in ways that lead to media use meaning different things to different people in different relationships at different times. The very existence of an interactive medium that connects people across space gives rise to new connections. Again we see that the amount of cues in a medium influence its use and perception in new relationships. Sparse cues may lead to overestimating one another's appeal early in relationships, and, in long-standing ones, they may lead to conflict. As relationships develop, we seek media that offer more cues to enrich our ties. As our ties become enriched, we seek multiple media through which to interact.

Qualities of media affect what we can use them to do in relationships. The size, portability, and discreetness of mobile phones makes them ideal for maintaining contact with loved ones, but can disrupt conversations with co-present partners. Asynchronous media that transcend space, such as email and SNSs, lend themselves to long-distance relational maintenance, yet also have local uses. The ease of relational creation and maintenance online allows people to expand their circles to maintain and include more weak ties, but can also serve to support strong ties.

Social influences are also essential in shaping how we use new media, with whom, and for what purposes. Relationship stage is a factor: early in relationships, we stick to the media in which we started. As relationships progress, we expand into others. Personality styles matter. Shy and anxious people may prefer online media, while those who are sociable to begin with may gravitate towards any medium that allows more opportunities to interact with others. Culture matters. Our national norms about behavior shape whether and when we text or call, and likely shape other media use as well. Peer group norms influence which behaviors we engage in and what we take for normal.

Over time it has become more normal in many cultures for people to meet and begin relationships online, but the norms that guide which media people use when and for what purposes are still unclear. Disagreements about appropriate partners for mediated encounters, the boundaries and expectations of online relationships, and the topics of mediated interaction have relational implications. People can't take for granted that the people with whom they have relationships share their attitudes. Figuring out when and how to use media to communicate with each other is part of figuring out what it means to relate well to others. Individuals have to find their own comfort levels in different media. Relational partners have to negotiate how they will use media with one another and what that says about their relationship, lest it lead to conflict. As societies, we will surely reach an operational consensus on these matters. But by then, there will be a new medium, and the process will begin again.

Conclusion: the myth of cyberspace

For those who vividly remember life without them, the internet and the mobile phone can still seem like they came out of nowhere and took over our lives. Those who grew up with them as part of their daily environments don't get what the fuss is about. There will be new communication technologies which today's children will find extraordinary and theirs will find mundane. This book was written for those who see the technologies it discusses as new and different, those who take them for granted, and those who will be thinking through technologies not yet invented.

When we first encounter interactive media yet to come, it will be almost entirely through the filters of communication. Our peers will talk about them. They will start turning up in news stories, movies, and television shows. We'll see ads for them. Maybe some of the people we know will use them. The topics these discourses stress, the tales they tell, and the impressions they pass along will be shaped by cultural forces far deeper and more powerful than a new machine or kind of interface. We all need to be savvy interpreters of the messages in popular media and interactions instead of taking them at face value.

The tendency is to think about new technologies deterministically, asking what they do to us, and whether that is good or bad. Thus we see concerns that mediated communication damages our ability to have face to face conversations, degrades language, undermines our connections to our communities and families, and replaces meaningful relationships with shallow substitutions. These perspectives co-exist in uneasy tensions with more optimistic scenarios in which mediation leads to closer families, more engaged citizens, more resources, and larger, better-connected social networks. Determinism can be recognized from its causal construction. The media are positioned as cause, the people are positioned as changed.

Yet people are adaptive, innovative, and influential in determining what technology is and will become. We use technology to suit our own aims and developers redesign and innovate to provide people with better ways to do the things they didn't expect us to do. Nowhere is this more obvious than when looking at social and emotional expression. Rather than be stymied by the lack of social cues inherent in text-only interaction, people innovated, making use of punctuation, capitalization, verbalization, and other tools to convey the social attitudes and feelings they wanted to impart. The internet was never envisioned as an interpersonal medium. Based on sheer features, at first blush it seemed poorly positioned to become one. But people took advantage of the affordances it did offer to make it into a social resource. Our drive to be social and find means of connecting with one another has been a guiding force in the internet's transformation from military and scientific network to staple of everyday life.

In 1984, William Gibson published *Neuromancer*, a futuristic computer-oriented science fiction novel in which he developed his neologism "cyberspace." He described it like this (ellipses in original):

> Cyberspace. A consensual hallucination experienced daily by billions of legitimate operators, in every nation, by children being taught mathematical concepts . . . A graphic representation of data abstracted from the banks of every computer in the human system. Unthinkable complexity. Line of light ranged in the nonspace of the mind, clusters and constellations of data. Like city lights, receding. (Gibson, 1984/2000: 51)

Gibson depicted his fictional cyberspace as a hallucinated "nonspace" like a never-ending city. The transition from real world to cyberspace, when you "hit the switch, was instantaneous" (Gibson 1984/2000: 55). For the book's protagonist, Case, a "cyberspace cowboy," cyberspace offered "the bodiless exultation" that gave him a reason to live (5–6). Though relatively few of the people who talk about new media have read *Neuromancer*, Gibson's prescient envisioning remains timely and influential. Throughout this book, we have seen many instances in which mediated interaction is treated as a "hallucination," bodiless, unreal, and seductive in its modern offering of the pioneering freedom of reinvention enjoyed by the cowboys of American mythos.

Deterministic orientations towards digital communication are often built on this sense of mediated communication as apart and different from real, embodied face to face interaction. Determinism is built on juxtaposing the online with the offline, comparing, contrasting, and looking for clear lines of influence. Yet, as we have seen throughout this book, the idea that these are separate realms does not hold up to scrutiny. There may be fantasy realms where people use the internet to create selves with no bearing on their offline selves, though, on close examination, even there the lines bleed. People do use the internet to create false identities. But these are the exceptions, not the norm. Taken as a whole, mediated communication is not a space, it is an additional tool people use to connect, one which can only be understood as deeply embedded in and influenced by the daily realities of embodied life.

Machines do have effects. The seven key concepts outlined in the introduction describe the primary affordances digital media offer, which reverberate throughout their use and consequences. Digital media vary in the extent to which they are interactive, storable, replicable, mobile, and how many people they can reach. They differ in whether they demand that people interact simultaneously or whether there can be time lags between messages. They offer widely varying ranges of social cues which, as we've seen, can affect self-presentation, honesty, relational development, and relational maintenance. Without the communication technologies we have now, we could not sustain the mobile and dispersed social and professional networks which many people take for granted. Just as we need critical tools for understanding the messages about new media, we need conceptual tools to look concretely at the qualities of a medium, consider how those qualities have played out in previous innovations, and understand how they are modified or expanded in combination in new media.

People also have effects on our personal connections. We need to understand the social dynamics into which technologies are introduced and in which they play out. Technologies do not arise from blank slates. They are first developed and deployed in social and cultural contexts. As adapters or non-adapters, throughout history, we come to media with social agendas, social commitments, and deeply ingrained social practices that are largely replicated and enacted through new technologies. We have seen this in the ways that relational contexts, gender, nationality, and group identities influence mediated behaviors and perceptions.

If we see digital connections as part and parcel of our everyday lives and social contexts, it's hard to see them as agents of radical transformation, either utopian or dystopian. There are no doors where we can check our personal, social, cultural, and historical identities and world views before entering. We are not free to create entirely new kinds of communication, selves, relationships, groups, networks, or worlds. Nor are we forced into an alternative world of shallow simulations of inauthentic message exchange that take us farther from one another. Digital media aren't saving us or ruining us. They aren't reinventing us. But they are changing the ways we relate to others and ourselves in countless, pervasive ways. We stay in touch with more people for longer and across greater distances. We find and share supportive resources we could never access before. We create groups and relationships that cross boundaries we could rarely span before. In some cases, we wander into bad circumstances we would have been better off without. In others we find new opportunities.

To ask whether mediated communication is as good as unmediated interaction, or whether online relationships are as good as unmediated relationships, is to miss the point. It is not a question of either/or, of one versus the other. It's a question of who's communicating, for what purposes, in what contexts, and what their expectations are. There are circumstances in which mediated interaction is preferable to face to face interaction, circumstances in which it is worse, and others when it's interchangeable. When people need more than mediation can provide, their use of the internet and telephones does not stop them from getting it. They just step away from the machines and get together, often using machines to coordinate that togetherness.

The research evidence and most of our personal experiences show that new media are not cyberspaces juxtaposed with the offline. My hope is that what eventually makes this book dated will be its evocation of a time when "online" and "offline" were still talked about in contrast to one another. But the history of new communication technologies suggests that the tendency to contrast and look for the influence of the mediated upon the embodied runs deep and will endure. New forms of mediation are disruptive in consistent ways throughout history. They evoke long-standing opposing tensions, or dialectics (Baxter & Montgomery, 2007). By transcending space, they enable us to connect with people who are not physically with us. Our bodies can be in one environment, yet our thoughts, feelings, and selves with someone elsewhere, positioning the body against the mind in a dualism that philosophers have been mulling for centuries. The tension between autonomy and interdependence, our desire to be left alone to be free to do what we like and our desire to need and be needed by others is exacerbated when new forms of technology allow both more control over one's own schedule and interactions and more continuous interconnection and accountability in our relationships. In all of our relationships, we need to find balances between how much we tell about ourselves, and how much we keep to ourselves. When new media collapse and expand our audiences, this challenge inherent in personal connections is amplified. When technologies afford us new capabilities, which we then depend on machines to attain, we must ask where the boundary lies between the people and their machines. In the digital age, just as at the dawn of writing, media evoke questions about what it means to be authentically human.

New media for personal connection make the social norms we take for granted visible and offer opportunities for changing them. This is hardly new to the digital age. Social norms have been diversifying and changing since they first appeared millennia ago, and will continue to evolve as long as there are people. Our need to sort through social evolution will continue, and technologies will remain opportune vehicles for triggering this reflection. I have emphasized the social shaping approach to understanding technology, recognizing that the machines have affordances that can push us in some directions rather than others, and that people have long- and short-term cultural, situational, and personal trajectories that shape the development, uses and consequences of technologies. This means that people have power. We can shape our personal connections through the ways we choose to understand and use embodied interaction, old media, and new media. The norms for appropriate use of communication media are in a continuous state of development. By being conscientious and aware of what media offer, what choices we make with them, and what consequences those choices have for us, we can intervene in and influence the process of norm development in our own relationships, our peer and familial groups, and our cultures. We can shape the contexts in which new media are developed and deployed.

The discourses around technology and the findings of research into its use and consequences tell us that, millennia after the inventions of the first communication technologies, we remain oriented towards preserving the authenticity of human connection and of ourselves. We develop and appropriate technologies as means of fostering meaningful personal connection. Along the way there are diversions, distractions, disasters and delights. What kinds of connections we foster with what kinds of people evolve. Like everyone who's come before us, we don't know what the future holds for our relationships. But when I look at how quickly and effectively people took over networks of digital signals that were never meant for sociability in the service of our need to connect, I am optimistic that we will navigate our way through innovation without losing hold of one another.

References

2birds1blog (2008) *The Twenty Male Poses of Facebook.* (Online) Available at www.2birds1blog.com/2008/04/20-male-poses-of-facebook.html (Accessed April 2, 2008).

Abbate, J. (1999) *Inventing the Internet.* Cambridge, MA: MIT Press.

Adelman, M. & Ahuvia, A. (1991) Mediated channels for mate seeking: a solution to involuntary singlehood? *Critical Studies in Mass Communication* 8, 273–89.

Altman, I. & Taylor, D. A. (1973) *Social Penetration: The Development of Interpersonal Relationships.* New York: Holt, Rinehart & Winston.

Andersen, P. & Guerrero, L. (1998) Principles of communication and emotion in social interaction. In P. Andersen & L. Guerrero (eds.) *Handbook of Communication and Emotion: Research, Theory, Applications, and Contexts.* San Diego, CA: Academic Press, pp. 49–99.

Anderson, J. Q. (2005) *Imagining the Internet.* Lanham, MA: Rowman & Littlefield.

Baker, A. (2008) Down the rabbit hole: the role of place in the initiation and development of online relationships. In A. Barak (ed.) *Psychological Aspects of Cyberspace: Theory, Research, Applications.* New York: Cambridge University Press, pp. 163–84.

Banet-Weiser, S. (2004) Surfin' the net: children, parental obsolesence, and citizenship. In M. Sturken, D. Thomas & S. J. Ball-Rokeach (eds.) *Technological Visions: The Hopes and Fears that Shape New Technologies.* Philadelphia, PA: Temple University Press, pp. 270–92.

Baron, N. S. (1998) Letters by phone or speech by other means: the linguistics of email. *Language and Communication* 18, 133–70.

—(2008) *Always On: Language in an Online and Mobile World.* New York: Oxford University Press.

—(1984) Computer mediated communication as a force in language change. *Visible Language* 18(2), 118–41.

—(2000) *Alphabet to Email: How Written English Evolved and Where It's Heading.* London: Routledge.

Baron, N. S. & Ling, R. (2003) IM and SMS: a linguistic comparison. Paper presented at Association of Internet Researchers Conference: Internet Research 4.0. Toronto, October.

Baron, N. S. & Hård af Segerstad, Y. (in press) Cross-cultural patterns in mobile phone use: public space and reachability in Sweden, the US, and Japan. *New Media & Society*.

Bartle, R. (2004) *Designing Virtual Worlds*. Berkley, CA: New Riders Publishing.

Baxter, L. & Montgomery, B. (2007) *Relating: Dialogues and Dialectics*. New York: Guilford Press.

Baym, N. K. (1995) The performance of humor in computer-mediated communication. *Journal of Computer-Mediated Communication* 1(2). (Online) Available at http://jcmc.indiana.edu/vol1/issue2/baym.html (accessed October 1, 2009).

—(1996) Agreement and disagreement in a computer-mediated group. *Research on Language and Social Interaction* 29, 315–46.

—(2000) *Tune In, Log On: Soaps, Fandom, and Online Community*. Sage, Thousand Oaks, CA.

—(2005) Online communication in close relationships: revealing what surveys obscure. In M. Consalve & M. Allen (eds.) *Internet Research Annual* Volume 2. Berlin: Peter Lang, pp. 51–62.

—(2007) The new shape of online community: the example of Swedish independent music fandom. *First Monday* 12(8). (Online) Available at http://firstmonday.org/htbin/cgiwrap/bin/ojs/index.php/fm/article/view/1978/1853 (accessed October 1, 2009).

Baym, N. K. & Burnett, R. (2009) Amateur experts: international fan labour in Swedish independent music. *International Journal of Cultural Studies* 12(5), 433–49.

Baym, N. K. & Ledbetter, A. (2009) Tunes that bind? Predicting friendship strength in a music-based social network. *Information, Community, & Society* 12(3), 408–27.

Baym, N. K., Zhang, Y. B. & Lin, M. (2004) Social interactions across media: interpersonal communication on the internet, telephone, and face to face. *New Media & Society* 6(3), 299–318.

Baym, N. K., Zhang, Y. B., Kunkel, A., Lin, M.-C. & Ledbetter, A. (2007) Relational quality and media use. *New Media & Society* 9(5), 735–52.

Benjamin, W. (2009 [1935]). *The Work of Art in the Age of Mechanical Reproduction*. New York: Classic Books America.

Bermudez, E. (2009) Death of blogger mom's daughter prompts outpouring from Internet community. *Los Angeles Times*, April 12.

(Online) Available at www.latimes.com/news/local/la-me-sickgirl12–
2009apr12,0,5058913.story (accessed September 29, 2009).

Berscheid, E., Dion, K., Hatfield, E. & Walster, G. W. (1971) Physical
attractiveness and dating choice, a test of the matching hypothesis.
Journal of Experimental Social Psychology 7, 173–89.

Bijker, W. E. & Law, J. (1992) *Shaping Technology / Building Society:
Studies in Sociotechnical Change.* Cambridge, MA: MIT Press.

Bijker, W. E., Hughes, T. P. & Pinch, T. J. (1987) *The Social Construction
of Technological Systems: New Directions in the Sociology and History of
Technology.* Cambridge, MA: MIT Press.

Boddy, W. (2004) *New Media and Popular Imagination: Launching Radio,
Television, and Digital Media in the United States.* Oxford: Oxford
University Press.

Bourdieu, P. (1984) *Distinction: A Social Critique of the Judgement of Taste.*
London: Routledge.

boyd, d. (2006) Friends, friendsters, and MySpace top 8: writing
community into being on social network sites. *First Monday* 11(12).
(Online) Available at http://firstmonday.org/htbin/cgiwrap/bin/
ojs/index.php/fm/article/view/1418/1336 (accessed October 1,
2009).

boyd, d. & Ellison, N. B. (2007) Social network sites: definition, history,
and scholarship. *Journal of Computer-Mediated Communication* 13(1).
(Online) Available at http://jcmc.indiana.edu/vol13/issue1/boyd.
ellison.html (accessed October 1, 2009).

boyd, d. & Heer, J. (2006) Profiles as conversation: networked identity
performance on Friendster. In *Proceedings of Thirty-Ninth Hawai'i
International Conference on System Sciences.* IEEE Press: Los Alamitos,
CA.

Burgess, J. & Green, J. (2009) *You Tube: Online Video and Participatory
Culture.* Cambridge: Polity Press.

Burleson, B. R. & Kunkel, A. (2006) Revisiting the different cultures
thesis: an assessment of sex differences and similarities in supportive
communication. In K. Dindia & D. Canary (eds.), *Sex Differences
and Similarities in Communication,* 2nd edn. Mahwah, NJ: Lawrence
Erlbaum, pp. 135–55.

Burleson, B. R. & MacGeorge, E. L. (2002) Supportive communication.
In M. L. Knapp & J. A. Daly (eds.) *Handbook of Interpersonal
Communication,* 3rd edn. Thousand Oaks, CA: Sage, pp. 374–424.

Byrne, D. N. (2007) Public discourse, community concerns, and civic
engagement: exploring black social networking traditions on
BlackPlanet.com. *Journal of Computer-Mediated Communication,* 13(1).

(Online) Available at http://jcmc.indiana.edu/vol13/issue1/byrne.
html (accessed October 1, 2009).

Campbell, S. & Russo, R. (2003) The social construction of mobile
telephony: an application of the social influence model to perceptions
and uses of mobile phones within personal communication networks.
Communication Monographs 70, 317–34.

Campbell, S. W. & Kwak, N. (2009) Political involvement in "mobilized"
society: the interactive relationships among mobile communication,
social network characteristics, and political life. Paper presented at
International Communication Association Pre-conference: Mobile
2.0: Beyond Voice? Chicago, May.

—(in press) Mobile communication and civic life: linking patterns of use
to civic and political engagement. *Journal of Communication.*

Carnevale, P. & Probst, T. M. (1997) Conflict on the internet. In: Kiesler,
S. (ed.) *Culture of the Internet.* Mahwah, NJ: Lawrence Erlbaum, pp.
233–55.

Carr, N. (2008). Is Google making us stupid? *The Atlantic*, July/August.
(Online) Available at www.theatlantic.com/doc/200807/google
(accessed September 29, 2009).

Cassell, J. & Cramer, M. (2007) Hi tech or high risk? Moral panics about
girls online. In T. MacPherson (ed.) *Digital Youth, Innovation, and the
Unexpected.* The MacArthur Foundation Series on Digital Media and
Learning. Cambridge, MA: MIT Press, pp. 53–75.

Castronova, E. (2004) The price of bodies: a hedonic pricing model of
avatar attributes in a synthetic world. *Kyklos* 57(2), 173–96.

Chan, D. K. S. & Cheng, G. H. L. (2004) A comparison of offline
and online friendship qualities at different stages of relationship
development. *Journal of Social and Personal Relationships* 21(3), 305–20.

Chayko, M. (2008) *Portable Communities: The Social Dynamics of Online
and Mobile Connectedness.* Albany, NY: SUNY Press.

Chen, W., Boase, J. & Wellman, B. (2002) The global villagers: comparing
internet users and uses around the world. In B. Wellman & C.
Haythornthwaite (eds.) *The Internet in Everyday Life.* Malden, MA:
Blackwell, pp. 74–113.

Cherny, L. (1999) *Conversation and Community: Chat in a Virtual World.*
Stanford: CSLI Publications.

Choi, J. H. (2006) Living in cyworld: contextualising cy-ties in South
Korea. In A. Bruns & J. Jacobs (eds.) *Use of Blogs.* New York: Peter
Lang, pp. 173–86.

Clark, L. S. (1998) Dating on the net: teens and the rise of "pure"
relationships. In S. Jones (ed.) *Cybersociety 2.0: Revisiting Computer-*

Mediated Communication and Community. Thousand Oaks, CA: Sage, pp. 159–83.

Cockroft, L. (2009) Facebook "enhances intelligence" but Twitter "diminishes it." claims psychologist. *Telegraph*, September 7. (Online) Available at www.telegraph.co.uk/technology/twitter/6147668/Facebook-enhances-intelligence-but-Twitter-diminishes-it-claims-psychologist.html (accessed September 29, 2009).

Cohen, S. (1972) *Folk Devils and Moral Panics*. London: MacGibbon and Kee.

Cole, J. (2000) *Surveying the Digital Future*. UCLA Center for Communication Policy. (Online) Available at www.digitalcenter.org/pages/site_content.asp?intGlobalId=20 (accessed October 1, 2009).

Coleman, J. S. (1988) Social capital in the creation of human capital. *The American Journal of Sociology* 94, S95–S120.

Copher, J. I., Kanfer, A. G. & Walker, M. B. (2002) Everyday communication patterns of heavy and light email users. In B. Wellman & C. Haythornthwaite (eds.) *The Internet in Everyday Life*. Malden, MA: Blackwell, pp. 263–90.

Culnan, M. J. & Markus, M. L. (1987) Information technologies. In F. M. Jablin, L. L. Putnam, H. Roberts & L. W. Porter (eds.) *Handbook of Organizational Computing: An Interdisciplinary Perspective*. Newbury Park, CA: Sage, pp. 420–43.

Curtis, P. (1997) Mudding: social phenomena in text-based virtual realities. In S. Kiesler (ed.) *Culture of the Internet*. Mahwah, NJ: Lawrence Erlbaum, pp. 121–42.

Cutrona, C. E. & Russell, D. W. (1990) Type of social support and specific stress: toward a theory of optimal matching. In B. R. Sarason, I. G. Sarason & G. R. Pearce (eds.) *Social Support: An Interactional View*. New York: Wiley, pp. 319–66.

Daft, R. L. & Lengel, R. H. (1984) Information richness: a new approach to managerial behaviour and organizational design. *Research in Organizational Behaviour* 6, 191–233.

Dahlgren, P. (2005) The internet, public spheres, and political communication: dispersion and deliberation. *Political Communication* 22, 147–62.

—(2009) *Media and Political Engagement: Citizens, Communication, and Democracy*. Cambridge: Cambridge University Press.

Danet, B. (1997) Books, letters, documents: the changing aesthetics of texts in late print culture. *Journal of Material Culture* 2(1), 5–38.

—(1998) Text as mask: gender, play and performance on the internet. In: Jones, S. G. (ed.) *Cybersociety 2.0: Computer-Mediated Communication and Community Revisited*. Thousand Oaks, CA: Sage, pp.129–58.

—(2001) *Cyberpl@y: Communicating Online.* Oxford, UK: Berg.

de Sola Pool, I. (1977). *The Social Impact of the Telephone.* Cambridge, MA: MIT Press.

Dimmick, J., Kline, S.L. and Stafford, L. (2000) The gratification niches of personal e-mail and the telephone: competition, displacement, and complementarity. *Communication Research* 27(2), 227–48.

Donath, J. (2007) Signals in social supernets. *Journal of Computer-Mediated Communication* 13(1). (Online) Available at http://jcmc.indiana.edu/vol13/issue1/donath.html (accessed October 1, 2009).

Donath, J. & boyd, d. (2004) Public displays of connection. *BT Technology Journal* 22(4), 71–82.

Douglas, S. (2004 [1999]) *Listening In: Radio and the American Imagination.* Minneapolis, MN: University of Minnesota Press.

Dundes, A. (1977) Who Are the Folk? In W. Bascom (ed.) *Frontiers of Folklore.* Boulder, CO: Westview Press, pp. 17–35.

Ellison, N., Heino, R. & Gibbs, J. (2006) Managing impressions online: self-presentation processes in the online dating environment. *Journal of Computer-Mediated Communication* 11(2). (Online) Available at http://jcmc.indiana.edu/vol11/issue2/ellison.html (accessed October 1, 2009).

Ellison, N., Steinfeld, C. & Lampe, C. (2007) The benefits of Facebook "friends": exploring the relationship between college students' use of online social networks and social capital. *Journal of Computer-Mediated Communication,* 12(4). (Online) Available at http://jcmc.indiana.edu/vol12/issue4/ellison.html (October 1, 2009).

—(2009). Connection strategies: relationship formation and maintenance on social network sites. Paper presented at International Communication Association Conference, Chicago, IL.

Fang, I. (2008) *Alphabet to Internet: Mediated Communication in Our Lives.* St Paul, MN: Rada Press.

Ferrara, K., Brunner, H. & Whittemore, G. (1991) Interactive written discourse as an emergent register. *Written Communication* 8, 8–34.

Finkenauer, C., Engels, R. C. M. E., Meeus, W. & Oosterwegel, A. (2002) Self and identity in early adolescence: the pains and gains of knowing who and what you are. In T. H. Brinthaupt & R. P. Lipka (eds.) *Understanding Early Adolescent Self and Identity: Applications and Interventions.* Albany, NY: SUNY Press, pp. 25–56.

Fiore, A. T. & Donath, J. S. (2005) Homophily in online dating: when do you like someone like yourself? Paper presented at ACM Computer–Human Interaction Conference, Portland, OR.

Fischer, C. S. (1992) *America Calling: A Social History of the Telephone to 1940.* Berkeley, CA: University of California Press.

Flanagin, A. J. & Metzger, M. J. (2001) Internet use in the contemporary media environment. *Human Communication Research* 27, 153–81.

Fono, D. & Raynes-Goldie, K. (2006) Hyperfriendship and beyond: friends and social norms on LiveJournal. In M. Consalvo & C. Haythornthwaite (eds.) *Internet Research Annual Volume 4: Selected Papers from the AOIR Conference.* New York: Peter Lang, pp. 91–103.

Fornås, J., Klein. K., Ladendorf, J., Sundén, J. & Sveningsson, M. (2002) Into digital borderlands. In J. Fornås, K. Klein, J. Ladendorf, J. Sunden & M. Sveningsson (eds.) *Digital Borderlands: Cultural Studies of Identity and Interactivity on the Internet.* New York: Peter Lang, pp. 1–47.

Fortunati, L. (2005) Is body to body communication still the prototype? *The Information Society* 21, 53–61.

Fragoso, S. (2006) WTF a crazy Brazilian invasion. In F. Sudweeks & H. Hrachovec (eds.) *Proceedings of CATaC 2006.* Murdoch, Australia: Murdoch University Press, pp. 255–74.

Fulk, J. (1993) Social construction of communication technology. *Academy of Management Journal* 36, 921–50.

Fulk, J. & Collins-Jarvis, L. (2001) Wired meetings: technological mediation of organizational gatherings. In F. M. Jablin & L. L. Putnam (eds.) *The New Handbook of Organizational Communication: Advances in Theory, Research and Methods.* Thousand Oaks, CA: Sage, pp. 624–63.

Fulk, J., Steinfield, C. W., Schmitz, J. & J. G. Power (1987) A social information processing model of media use in organizations. *Communication Research* 14(5), 529–52.

Gajjala, R. (2004) *Cyberselves: Feminist Ethnographies of South Asian Women.* London: Altamira Press.

Gergen, K. J. (1991) *The Saturated Self: Dilemmas of Identity in Contemporary Life.* New York: Basic Books.

—(2002) The challenge of absent presence. In J. E. Katz & M. Aakhus (eds.) *Perpetual Contact: Mobile Communication, Private Talk, Public Performance.* Cambridge: Cambridge University Press, pp. 227–41.

—(2008) Mobile communication and the transformation of the democratic process. In J. E. Katz (ed.) *Handbook of Mobile Communication Studies.* Cambridge, MA: MIT Press, pp. 297–310.

Gibson, W. (1984/2000) *Neuromancer,* ACE edition. New York: The Berkley Publishing Group.

Giddens, A. (1991) *Modernity and Self-Identity: Self and Location in the Late Modern Age.* Palo Alto, CA: Stanford University Press.

—(1993) *The Transformation of Intimacy.* Palo Alto, CA: Stanford University Press.

Gilbert, E., Karahalios, K. & Sandvig, C. (2008) The network in the garden: an empirical analysis of social media in rural life. Paper presented at CHI 2008 conference. Florence, Italy, April.

Goffman, E. (1959) *The Presentation of Self in Everyday Life*. Garden City, NY: Doubleday.

—(1963) *Behavior in Public Places: Notes on the Social Organization of Gatherings*. New York: Free Press.

—(1971) *Relations in Public: Microstudies of the Public Order*. New York: Basic Books.

Golder, S. A., Wilkinson, D. & Huberman, B. A. (2007) Rhythms of social interaction: messaging within a massive online network. In C. Steinfield, B. Pentland, M. Ackerman & N. Contractor (eds.) *Proceedings of Third International Conference on Communities and Technologies*. London: Springer, pp. 41–66.

Goodwin, C. (1981) *Conversational Organization: Interaction between Speakers and Hearers*. New York: Academic Press.

Granovetter, M. S. (1973) The strength of weak ties. *American Journal of Sociology* 78, 1160–80.

Gray, M. L. (2009) *Out in the Country: Youth, Media and Queer Visibility in Rural America*. New York: New York University Press.

Gross, R. & Acquisti, A. (2005) Information revelation and privacy in online social networks. In *Proceedings of the ACM WPES'05*. Alexandria, VA: ACM Press. pp. 71–80.

Gurak, L. L. (1997) *Persuasion and Privacy in Cyberspace: The Online Protests over Lotus MarketPlace and the Clipper Chip*. New Haven, CT: Yale University Press.

—(2001) *Cyberliteracy: Navigating the Internet with Awareness*. New Haven, CT: Yale University Press.

Haddon, L. (2006) The contribution of domestication research. *The Information Society* 22(4), 195–204.

Hafner, K. (1998) *Where Wizards Stay Up Late: The Origins of the Internet*. New York: Simon & Schuster.

Hampton, K. N. (in press) Internet use and the concentration of disadvantage: glocalization and the urban underclass. *Journal of Communication*.

Hampton, K. N. & Wellman, B. (2003) Neighboring in Netville: how the internet supports community and social capital in a wired suburb. *City & Community* 2(4), 277–311.

Hampton, K. N., Livio, O. & Sessions L. (in press) The social life of wireless urban spaces: internet use, social networks, and the public realm. *Journal of Communication*.

Hancock, J. T., Thom-Santelli, J. & Ritchie, T. (2004) Deception and design: the impact of communication technology on lying behavior. Paper presented at CHI 2004 conference, Vienna, Austria, April.

Hansen, D., Ackerman, M., Resnick, P. & Munson, S. (2007) Virtual community maintenance with a repository. In *Proceedings of ASIS&T 2007*. Milwaukee, WI.

Haraway, D. (1990) A manifesto for cyborgs: science, technology, and socialist feminism in the 1980s. In L. J. Nicholson (ed.) *Feminism/ Postmodernism*. London: Routledge, pp. 190–233.

Hård af Segerstad, Y. (2005) Language use in Swedish mobile text messaging. In R. Ling & P. Pederson (eds.) *Mobile Communications: Renegotiations of the Social Sphere*. London: Springer, pp. 313–34.

Hargittai, E. (2002) Second-level digital divide: differences in people's online skills. *First Monday* 7(4). (Online) Available at http:// firstmonday.org/htbin/cgiwrap/bin/ojs/index.php/fm/article/ view/942/864 (accessed October 1, 2009).

Hargittai, E. & Hinnant, A. (2008) Digital inequality: differences in young adults' use of the internet. *Communication Research* 35(5), 602–21.

Hartelius, E. (2005) A content-based taxonomy of blogs and the formation of a virtual community. *Kaleidoscope: A Graduate Journal of Qualitative Communication Research* 4, 71–91.

Haythornthwaite, C. (2002) Strong, weak, and latent ties and the impact of new media. *Information Society* 18, 385–401.

—(2005) Social networks and Internet connectivity effects. *Information, Communication, & Society* 8(2), 125–47.

Haythornthwaite, C. & Wellman, B. (2002) The internet in everyday life: an introduction. In B. Wellman & C. Haythornthwaite (eds.) *The Internet in Everyday Life*. Malden, MA: Blackwell.

Healy, D. (1997) Cyberspace and place: the internet as middle landscape on the electronic frontier. In D. Porter (ed.) *Internet Culture*. New York: Routledge. pp. 55–71.

Henderson, S. & Gilding, M. (2004) "I've never clicked this much with anyone in my life": trust and hyperpersonal communication in online friendships. *New Media & Society* 6: 487–506.

Herring, S. (1996) Posting in a different voice: gender and ethics in computer-mediated communication. In C. Ess (ed.) *Philosophical Approaches to Computer-Mediated Communication*. Albany, NY: SUNY Press, pp. 115–45.

—(2001) Computer-mediated discourse. In D. Schiffrin, D. Tannen & H. E. Hamiton (eds.) *The Handbook of Discourse Analysis*. Malden, MA: Blackwell, pp. 612–34.

Herring, S. & Danet, B. (2003) Editor's introduction: the multilingual internet. *Journal of Computer-Mediated Communication* 9(1). (Online) Available at http://jcmc.indiana.edu/vol9/issue1/intro.html (accessed October 1, 2009).

Herring, S. C., Paolillo, J. C., Ramos-Vielba, I., et al. (2007) Language networks on LiveJournal. In *Proceedings of the Fortieth Hawaii International Conference on System Sciences*. Los Alamitos, CA. (Online) Available at http://ella.slis.indiana.edu/~herring/hicss07.pdf (accessed October 1, 2009).

Hijazi-Omari, H. & Ribak, R. (2008) Playing with fire: on the domestication of the mobile phone among Palestinian girls in Israel. *Information, Communication & Society* 11, 149–66.

Hiltz, S. R. & Turoff, M. (1978) *The Network Nation: Human Communication via Computer*. Reading, MA: Addison-Wesley.

Horrigan, J. & Rainie L. (2002) The broadband difference: how online behavior changes with high-speed Internet connections. Pew Internet and American Life Project. (Online) Available at www.pewinternet. org/Reports/2002/The-Broadband-Difference-How-online-behavior-changes-with-highspped-Internet-connections.aspx (accessed 1 October 2009).

Howard, P. N., Rainie, L. & Jones, S. (2001) Days and nights on the internet: the impact of a diffusing technology. *American Behavioral Scientist* 45(3), 383–404.

Humphreys, L. (2005) Cell phones in public: social interactions in a wireless era. *New Media & Society* 7(6), 810–33.

—(2007) Mobile social networks and social practice: a case study of Dodgeball. *Journal of Computer-Mediated Communication*, 13(1). (Online) Available at http://jcmc.indiana.edu/vol13/issue1/humphreys.html (accessed October 1, 2009).

Institut za Etnologiju i Folkloristiku (2004) *Etnografije interneta*. Zagreb: Ibis grafika.

International Telecommunications Union (2009) Measuring the information society. (Online) Available at www.itu.int/ITU-D/ict/publications/idi/2009/index.html (accessed September 17, 2009).

Internet Safety Technical Task Force (2008) *Enhancing Child Safety & Online Technologies*. Berkman Center for Internet & Society, Cambridge, MA: Harvard University. (Online) Available at http://cyber.law.harvard.edu/research/isttf (accessed September 17, 2009).

Ishii, K. (2006) Implications of mobility: the uses of personal communication media in everyday life. *Journal of Communication* 56(2), 346–65.

Ito, M. (1997) Virtually embodied: the reality of fantasy in a multi-user dungeon. In: Porter, D. (ed.) *Internet Culture*. New York: Routledge, pp. 87–110.

Jenkins, H. (2006) *Convergence Culture: Where Old and New Media Collide*. New York: New York University Press.

Jung, J., Qiu, J. & Kim, Y. C. (2001) Internet connectedness and inequality: beyond the digital divide. *Communication Research* 28(4), 507–35.

Kasesniemi, E. & Rautiainen, P. (2002) Mobile culture of children and teenagers in Finland. In J. E Katz & M. Aakhus (eds.) *Perpetual Contact: Mobile Communication, Private Talk, Public Performance*. Cambridge: Cambridge University Press, pp, 170–92.

Katz, J. E. & Aakhus, M. (2002) Introduction: framing the issues. In J. E Katz & M. Aakhus (eds.) *Perpetual Contact: Mobile Communication, Private Talk, Public Performance*. Cambridge: Cambridge University Press, pp. 1–13.

Katz, J. E. & Aspden, P. (1997) A nation of strangers? *Communications of the ACM* 40(12, December), 81–6.

Katz, J. E. & Rice, R. E. (2002) Project Syntopia: social consequences of internet use. *IT & Society* 1(1), 166–79.

Kendall, L. (2002) *Hanging out in the Virtual Pub: Masculinities and Relationships Online*. Berkeley, CA: University of California Press.

Kibby, M. (2010) The gendered practice of fandom online. In R. Lind (ed.) *Race/Gender/Media: Considering Diversity across Audiences, Content and Producers*, 2nd edn., Chicago: AB-Longman, pp. 237–44.

Kiesler, S., Siegel, J. & McGuire, T. W. (1984) Social psychological aspect of computer-mediated communication. *American Psychologist* 39, 1123–34.

Kim, K.-H. & Yun, H. (2007) Cying for me, cying for us: relational dialectics in a Korean social network site. *Journal of Computer-Mediated Communication* 13(1). (Online) Available at http://jcmc. indiana.edu/vol13/issue1/kim.yun.html (accessed October 1, 2009).

Knapp, M. L. (1983) Dyadic relationship development. In J. M. Wiemann & R. P. Harrison (eds.) *Nonverbal Interaction*. Beverly Hills, CA: Sage.

Kollock, P. (1999) The economies of online cooperation: gifts and public goods in cyberspace. In M. Smith & P. Kollock (eds.) *Communities in Cyberspace*. New York: Routledge, pp. 220–42.

Koutsogiannis, D. & Mitsikopoulou, B. (2003) Greek and Greeklish: trends and discourses of "glocalness". *Journal of Computer-Mediated Communication* 9(1). (Online) Available at http://jcmc.indiana.edu/ vol9/issue1/kouts_mits.html (accessed October 1, 2009).

Kraut, R., Mukhopadhyay, T., Szczypula, J., Kiesler, S. & Scherlis, B. (2000) Information and communication: alternative uses of the Internet in households. *Information Systems Research* 10, 287–303.

Kunkel, A. W. & Burleson, B. R. (1999) Assessing explanations for sex differences in emotional support: a test of the different cultures and skill specialization accounts. *Human Communication Research* 25, 307–40.

Lampe, C., Ellison, N. & Steinfeld, C. (2007) A familiar Face(book): profile elements as signals in an online social network. In *Proceedings of Conference on Human Factors in Computing Systems*. New York: ACM Press, pp. 435–44.

Languages (n.d.). NITLE Blog Census. (Online) Available at www.hirank.com/semantic-indexing-project/census/lang.html (accessed September 15, 2009).

Larsen, M. C. (2007) Understanding social networking: on young people's construction and co-construction of identity online. Paper presented at Internet Research 8.0 conference, Vancouver, BC.

Larson, K. A. (2003) The influence of gender and topic on nonverbal communication in online discussion boards. Unpublished undergraduate honors thesis, Department of Communication Studies, University of Kansas, Lawrence, KS.

Lave, J., & Wenger, E. (1991) *Situated Learning: Legitimate Peripheral Participation*. New York: Cambridge University Press.

Lea, M. & Spears, R. (1991) Computer-mediated communication, de-individuation and group decision-making. *International Journal of Man-Machine Studies Special Issue: Computer-Supported Cooperative Work and Groupware* 34, 283–301.

Lea, M., O'Shea, T., Fung, P. & Spears, R. (1992) "Flaming" in computer-mediated communication: observations, explanations, implications. In M. Lea (ed.) *Contexts of Computer-Mediated Communication*. London: Harvester Wheatsheaf, pp. 89–112.

Lenhart, A. & Madden, M. (2007). Teens, privacy, & online social networks. Pew Internet and American Life Project, April 18. (Online) Available at www.pewinternet.org/Reports/2007/Teens-Privacy-and-Online-Social-Networks.aspx?r=1 (accessed October 1, 2009).

Licoppe, C. & Heurtin J. P. (2002) France: preserving the image. In: Katz, J. E. & M. Aakhus (eds.) *Perpetual Contact: Mobile Communication, Private Talk, Public Performance*. Cambridge: Cambridge University Press, pp. 94–109.

Lievrouw, L. A. (2006) New media design and development: diffusion of innovations v social shaping of technology. In L. A. Lievrouw &

S. Livingston (eds.) *The Handbook of New Media, Updated Student Edition*. London: Sage, pp. 246–65.

Ling, R. (2004) *The Mobile Connection: The Cell Phone's Impact on Society*. San Francisco: Elsevier.

—(2005) The socio-linguistics of SMS: an analysis of SMS use by a random sample of Norwegians. In R. Ling & P. Pederson (eds.) *Mobile Communications: Renegotiations of the Social Sphere*. London: Springer, pp. 335–49.

Ling, R. & Yttri, B. (2002) Hyper-coordination via mobile phones in Norway. In J. E. Katz & M. Aakhus (eds.) *Perpetual Contact: Mobile Communication, Private Talk, Public Performance*. Cambridge: Cambridge University Press, pp. 139–69.

Lister, M., Dovey, J., Giddings, S., Grant, I. & Kelly, K. (2003) *New Media: A Cultural Introduction*. London: Routledge.

Liu, H. (2007) Social network profiles as taste performances. *Journal of Computer-Mediated Communication* 13(1). (Online) Available at http://jcmc.indiana.edu/vol13/issue1/liu.html (accessed October 1, 2009].

Liu, H., Maes, P. & Davenport, G. (2006) Unraveling the taste fabric of social networks. *International Journal on Semantic Web and Information Systems* 2(1), 42–71.

Livingstone, S. (2005) Mediating the public/private boundary at home: children's use of the Internet for privacy and participation. *Journal of Media Practice* 6(1), 41–51.

—(2008) Internet literacy: young people's negotiation of new online opportunities. In T. McPherson (ed.) *Unexpected Outcomes and Innovative Uses of Digital Media by Youth*. MacArthur Foundation Series on Digital Media and Learning. Cambridge, MA: MIT Press, pp. 101–21.

Lockard, J. (1997) Progressive politics, electronic individualism and the myth of virtual community. In D. Porter (ed.) *Internet Culture*. New York: Routledge, pp. 219–32.

Mankoff, R. (ed.) (2004) *The Complete Cartoons of the New Yorker*. New York: Black Dog and Leventhal Publishers.

Markus, L. (1994) Finding the happy medium: explaining the negative effects of electronic communication on social life at work. *ACM Transactions on Information Systems* 12, 119–49.

Marvin, C. (1988) *When Old Technologies Were New*. New York: Oxford University Press.

—(2004) Peaceable kingdoms and new information technology: prospects for the nation-state. In M. Sturken, D. Thomas & S. J. Ball-Rokeach (eds.) *Technological Visions: The Hopes and Fears that Shape New Technologies*. Philadelphia, PA: Temple University Press, pp. 240–54.

Matei, S. & Ball-Rokeach, S. (2002) Belonging in geographic, ethnic, and internet spaces. In B. Wellman & C. Haythornthwaite (eds.) *The Internet in Everyday Life.* Malden, MA: Blackwell, pp. 404–30.

Matzat, U. (2004) Cooperation and community on the internet: past issues and present perspectives for theoretical–empirical internet research. *Analyse & Kritik* 26(1), 63–90.

Mayer, A. & Puller, S. L. (2007) The old boy (and girl) network: social network formation on university campuses. *Journal of Public Economics* 92, 329–47.

McKenna, K. Y. A. & Bargh, J. A. (1998) Coming out in the age of the internet: identity "demarginalization" from virtual group participation. *Journal of Personality & Social Psychology* 74, 681–94.

McKenna, K. Y. A., Green, A. S. & Gleason, M. E. J. (2002) Relationship formation on the internet: what's the big attraction? *Journal of Social Issues* 58(1), 9–31.

McLaughlin, M. L., Osborne, K. K. and Smith, C. B. (1995) Standards of conduct on Usenet. In S. Jones (ed.) *Cybersociety: Computer-Mediated Communication and Community.* Thousand Oaks, CA: Sage, pp. 90–111.

Mehrabian, A. (1971) *Silent Messages.* Belmont, CA: Wadsworth.

Mesch, G. and Talmud, I. (2006) The quality of online and offline relationships. *The Information Society* 22, 137–48.

Mesch, G. S. and Levanon, Y. (2003) Community networking and locally based social ties in two suburban localities. *City and Community* 2, 335–51.

Meyrowitz, J. (1985) *No Sense of Place: The Impact of Electronic Media on Social Behavior.* New York: Oxford University Press.

Miller, D. & Slater, D. (2000) *The Internet: An Ethnographic Approach.* Oxford: Berg.

Miniwatts Marketing Group (2009) World internet penetration rates by geographic regions. (Online) Available at www.internetworldstats. com/stats.htm (accessed September 17, 2009).

Mitra, A. (1997) Virtual commonality: looking for India on the internet. In S. Jones (ed.) *Virtual Culture.* Newbury Park, CA: Sage, pp. 55–79.

Myers, D. (1987a) A new environment for communication play: online play. In G. A. Fine (ed.) *Meaningful Play, Playful Meaning.* Champaign, IL: Human Kinetics Publishers, pp. 231–45.

—(1987b) "Anonymity is part of the magic": individual manipulation of computer-mediated communication contexts. *Qualitative Sociology* 19(3), 251–66.

Nakamura, L. (2002) *Cybertypes: Race, Ethnicity, and Identity on the Internet.* New York: Routledge.

Nie, N. H. & Erbring, L. (2000) *Internet and Society: A Preliminary Report*, February 17. Palo Alto, CA: Stanford Institute for the Quantitative Study of Society. (Online) Available at www.stanford.edu/group/ siqss/ (accessed October 1, 2009).

Nie, N. H., Hillygus, D. S. & Erbring, L. (2002) Internet use, interpersonal relations and sociability: a time diary study. In B. Wellman & C. Haythornthwaite (eds.) *The Internet in Everyday Life*. Malden, MA: Blackwell, pp. 215–43.

Norris, P. (2001) *Digital Divide: Civic Engagement, Information Poverty and the Internet*. Cambridge: Cambridge University Press.

Nye, D. E. (1997) *Narratives and Spaces: Technology and the Construction of American Culture*. New York: Columbia University Press.

—(2004) Technological prediction. In: Sturken, M. Thomas, D. & Ball-Rokeach, S. J. (eds.) *Technological Visions: The Hopes and Fears that Shape New Technologies*. Philadelphia, PA: Temple University Press, pp. 159–76.

O'Sullivan, P. B. (2000) What you don't know won't hurt ME: impression management functions of communication channels in relationships. *Human Communication Research* 26(3), 403–31.

O'Sullivan, P. B., Hunt, S. & Lippert, L. (2004) Mediated immediacy: a language of affiliation in a technological age. *Journal of Language and Social Psychology* 23, 464–90.

OkCupid (2009). Online dating advice: exactly what to say in a first message. *OkTrends Blog*, September 14. (Online) Available at http:// blog.okcupid.com/index.php/2009/09/14/online-dating-advice-exactly-what-to-say-in-a-first-message/ (accessed September 14, 2009).

Oksman, V. & Turtiainen, J. (2004) Mobile communication as a social stage: meanings of mobile communication in everyday life among teenagers in Finland. *New Media Society* 6, 319–39.

Oldenburg, R. (1989) *The Great Good Place: Cafes, Coffee Shops, Community Centers, Beauty Parlors, General Stores, Bars, Hangouts, and How They Get You Through the Day*. New York: Paragon House.

Ong, W. J. (1982) *Orality and Literacy: The Technologizing of the World*. New York: Routledge.

Orleans, M. & Laney, M. C. (2000) Children's computer use in the home: isolation or sociation? *Social Science Computer Review* 18(1), 56–72.

Papacharissi, Z. (2002) The presentation of self in virtual life: characteristics of personal home pages. *Journalism and Mass Communication Quarterly* 79(3), 643–60.

Parks, M. (2006) *Personal Relationships and Personal Networks*. Mahwah, NJ: Lawrence Erlbaum.

Parks, M. R. & Floyd, K. (1996) Making friends in cyberspace. *Journal of Communication* 46(1), 80–97.

Parks, M. R. & Roberts, L. D. (1998) "Making MOOsic": the development of personal relationships online and a comparison to their offline counterparts. *Journal of Social and Personal Relationships* 15(4), 517–37.

Philipsen, G. (1992) Speaking culturally: explorations in social communication. Albany, NY: SUNY Press.

Plato (2008[360 BCE]) *Phaedrus*. Charleston, SC: Forgotten Books.

Postmes, T. & Baym, N. K. (2005) Intergroup dimensions of the internet. In: Harwood, J. & Giles, H. (eds.), *Intergroup Communication: Multiple Perspectives*. New York: Peter Lang, pp. 213–38.

Preece, J. & Ghozati, K. (1998) In search of empathy online: a review of 100 online communities. In: *Proceedings of the 1998 Association for Information Systems Americas Conference*. Baltimore, MD: Association for Information Systems. pp. 92–4.

Preece, J. & Maloney-Krichmar, D. (2003) Online communities. In: Jacko, J. & Sears, A. (eds.) *Handbook of Human–Computer Interaction*. Mahwah, NJ: Lawrence Erlbaum, pp. 596–620.

Preece, J., Nonnecke, B. & Andrews, D. (2004) The top 5 reasons for lurking: improving community experiences for everyone. *Computers in Human Behavior* 20(2), 201–23.

Puro, J.-P. (2002) Finland: A mobile culture. In J. E. Katz & M. Aakhus (eds.) *Perpetual Contact: Mobile Communication, Private Talk, Public Performance*. Cambridge: Cambridge University Press, pp. 19–29.

Putnam, R. (1995) Bowling alone: America's declining social capital. *Journal of Democracy* 6(1), 65–78.

—(2000) *Bowling Alone: The Collapse and Revival of American Community*. New York: Simon & Schuster.

Quan-Haase, A., Wellman, B., Witte, J. & Hampton, K. N. (2002) Capitalizing on the net: social contact, civic engagement, and sense of community. In B. Wellman & C. Haythornthwaite (eds.) *The Internet in Everyday Life*. Malden, MA: Blackwell, pp. 291–324.

Rafaeli, S. & Sudweeks, F. (1997) Networked interactivity. *Journal of Computer-Mediated Communication* 2(4). (Online) Available at http://jcmc.indiana.edu/vol2/issue4/rafaeli.sudweeks.html (accessed October 1, 2009).

Rainie, L., Lenhart, A., Fox, S., Spooner, T. & Horrigan, J. (2000) Tracking online life: how women use the internet to cultivate relationships with family and friends. Pew Internet and American Life Project. (Online) Available at www.pewinternet.org/Reports/2000/Tracking-Online-Life.aspx (accessed October 1, 2009).

Rakow, L. (1992) *Gender on the Line: Women, the Telephone and Community Life*. Chicago: University of Illinois Press.

Rawlins, W. K. (1992) *Friendship Matters: Communication, Dialectics and the Life Course*. New York: Aldine de Gruyter.

Rheingold, H. (1993) *The Virtual Community: Homesteading on the Electronic Frontier*. Reading, MA: Addison-Wesley.

Rice, R. E. (1984) Mediated group communication. In R. E. Rice and associates (eds.) *The New Media: Communication, Research, and Technology*. Beverly Hills, CA: Sage, 129–56.

—(1989) Issues and concepts in research on computer-mediated communication systems. In J. A. Anderson (ed.) *Communication Yearbook Volume 12*. Newbury Park, CA: Sage, pp. 436–76.

Rice, R. E. & Love, G. (1987) Electronic emotion: socioemotional content in a computer-mediated communication network. *Communication Research* 14(1), 85–108.

Robinson, J. P., Kestnbaum, M., Neustadtl, A. & Alvarez, A. S. (2002) The internet and other uses of time. In B. Wellman & C. Haythornthwaite (eds.) *The Internet in Everyday Life*. Malden, MA: Blackwell, pp. 244–62.

Rutter, J. & Smith, G. W. H. (1999) Presenting the offline self in an everyday online environment. Paper presented at Identities in Action Conference. University of Wales, December.

Sarch, A. (1993) Making the connection: single women's use of the telephone in dating relationships with men. *Journal of Communication* 42, 128–44.

Savicki, V., Lingenfelter, D. & Kelley, M. (1996) Gender language style and group composition in internet discussion groups. *Journal of Computer-Mediated Communication* 2(3). (Online) Available at http://jcmc.indiana.edu/vol2/issue3/ (accessed October 1, 2009).

Schegloff, E. (2002) Beginnings in the telephone. In J. E. Katz & M. Aakhus (eds.) *Perpetual Contact: Mobile Communication, Private Talk, Public Performance*. Cambridge: Cambridge University Press, pp. 284–300.

Schuler, D. (1996) *New Community Networks: Wired for Change*. Reading, MA: Addison-Wesley.

Shea, V. (n.d.). Netiquette: flame wars. (Online) Available at www.albion.com/bookNetiquette/0963702513p73.html (accessed October 1, 2009).

Short, J., Williams, E. & Christie, B. (1976) *The Social Psychology of Telecommunications*. Chichester, UK: Wiley.

Silver, D. (2000) Margins in the wires: looking for race, gender and
    sexuality in the Blacksburg Electronic Village. In B. Kolko, L. Nakamura
    & G. B. Rodman, *Race in Cyberspace*. New York: Routledge, pp. 133–50.
Silverstone, R., Hirsch, E. & Morley, D. (1992) Information and
    communication technologies and the moral economy of the
    household. In R. Silverstone & E. Hirsch (eds.) *Consuming
    Technologies: Media and Information in Domestic Spaces*. London:
    Routledge, pp. 9–17.
Smith, A., Schlozman, K. L., Verba, S. & Brady, H. (2009) The internet
    and civic engagement. Pew Internet and American Life Project.
    (Online) Available at www.pewinternet.org/Reports/2009/15--The-
    Internet-and-Civic-Engagement.aspx (accessed October 1, 2009).
Snyder, J., Carpenter, D. & Slauson, G. J. (2006) MySpace.com: a social
    networking site and social contract theory. In *Proceedings of ISECON
    2006*. (Online) Available at http://isedj.org/isecon/2006/3333/
    ISECON.2006.Snyder.pdf (accessed October 1, 2009).
Sparta Networks (n.d.) Lincoln uses Sparta social networks to help make
    dreams come true. (Online) Available at www.spartasocialnetworks.
    com/clients/case-studies/case-study-lincoln/ (accessed October 1,
    2009).
Spears, R. & Lea, M. (1992) Social influence and the influence of the
    "social" in computer-mediated communication. In M. Lea (ed.)
    Contexts of Computer-Mediated Communication. Hemel Hempstead:
    Harvester Wheatsheaf, pp. 30–65.
Spigel, L. (1992) *Make Room for TV: Television and the Family Ideal in
    Postwar America*. Chicago: University of Chicago Press.
—(2004) Portable TV: studies in domestic space travels. In M. Sturken,
    D. Thomas & S. J. Ball-Rokeach (eds.) *Technological Visions: The Hopes
    and Fears that Shape New Technologies*. Philadelphia, PA: Temple
    University Press, pp. 110–44.
Sproull, L. & Kiesler, S. (1991) *Connections: New Ways of Working in the
    Networked Organization*. Cambridge, MA: MIT Press.
Stafford, L., Kline, S. L. & Dimmick, J. (1999) Home e-mail: relational
    maintenance and gratification opportunities. *Journal of Broadcasting &
    Electronic Media* 43(4), 659–69.
Standage, T. (1998) *The Victorian Internet*. New York: Berkley.
Steinkuehler, C. A. & Williams, D. (2006) Where everybody knows your
    (screen) name: online games as "third places". *Journal of Computer-
    Mediated Communication*, 11(4). (Online) Available at http://jcmc.
    indiana.edu/vol11/issue4/steinkuehler.html (accessed October 1,
    2009).

Stephenson, N. (1992) *Snow Crash.* New York: Spectra.

Stivale, C. (1997) Spam: heteroglossia and harassment in cyberspace. In D. Porter (ed.) *Internet Culture.* New York: Routledge, pp. 133–44.

Stoll, C. (1995). *Silicon Snake Oil: Second Thoughts on the Information Highway.* New York: Doubleday.

Stone, A. R. (1995) *The War of Desire and Technology at the Close of the Mechanical Age.* Cambridge, MA: MIT Press.

Stratton, J. (1997) Cyberspace and the globalization of culture. In D. Porter (ed.) *Internet Culture.* New York: Routledge, pp. 253–76.

Stross, C. (2007) *Halting State.* New York: Berkley Publishing Group.

Sturken, M. & Thomas, D. (2004) Introduction: technological visions and the rhetoric of the new. In M. Sturken, D. Thomas & S. J. Ball-Rokeach (eds.) *Technological Visions: The Hopes and Fears that Shape New Technologies.* Philadelphia, PA: Temple University Press, pp. 1–18.

Sudweeks, F., McLaughlin, M. & Rafaeli, S. (1998) *Networks and Netplay: Virtual Groups on the Internet.* Cambridge, MA: MIT Press.

Tajfel, H. & Turner, J. C. (1986) The social identity theory of intergroup behavior. In S. Worchel & W. G. Austin (eds.), *The Psychology of Intergroup Relations.* Chicago: Nelson-Hall, pp. 7–24.

Thomas, D. (2004) Rethinking the cyberbody: hackers, viruses, and cultural anxiety. In M. Sturken, D. Thomas & S. J. Ball-Rokeach (eds.) *Technological Visions: The Hopes and Fears that Shape New Technologies.* Philadelphia, PA: Temple University Press, pp. 219–39.

Thomas, O. (2009) Jerry Yang's incompetent layoff memo. *Valleywag.* (Online) Available at http://valleywag.com/5106683/jerry-yangs-incompetent-layoff-memo (accessed October 1, 2009).

Thurlow, C., Lengel, L. & Tomic, A. (2004) *Computer-Mediated Communication: Social Interaction and the Internet.* Los Angeles: Sage.

Translate to Success (2009) Internet language use statistics. (Online) Available at www.translate-to-success.com/internet-language-use.html (accessed September 20, 2009).

Turkle, S. (1996) *Life on the Screen: Identity in the Age of the Internet.* New York: Simon & Schuster.

(1997) Constructions and reconstructions of self in virtual reality: playing in the MUDs. In S. Kiesler (ed.) *Culture of the Internet.* Mahwah, NJ: Lawrence Erlbaum, pp. 143–55.

(2004) "Spinning" technology: what we are not thinking about when we are thinking about computers. In M. Sturken, D. Thomas & S. J. Ball-Rokeach (eds.) *Technological Visions: The Hopes and Fears that Shape New Technologies.* Philadelphia, PA: Temple University Press, pp. 19–33.

S. Tuszynski (dir.) (2007) *IRL: In Real Life*. (Film) DL Films.

Twitter tweets are 40% "babble" (2009). *BBC News*, August 19. (Online) Available at http://news.bbc.co.uk/2/hi/technology/8204842.stm (accessed September 29, 2009).

Ullman, E. (1997) *Close to the Machine: Technophilia and its Discontents*. San Francisco: City Lights Books.

UN (2001) Human Development Report. *Making New Technologies Work for Human Development*. (Online) Available at http://hdr.undp.org/en/reports/global/hdr2001/ (accessed September 29, 2009).

Walker, R. (2008) *Buying In: The Secret Dialogue between What We Buy and Who We Are*. New York: Random House.

Walther, J. B. (1992) Interpersonal effects in computer-mediated interaction. *Communication Research* 19(1), 52–90.

—(1994) Anticipated ongoing interaction versus channel effects on relational communication in computer-mediated interaction. *Human Communication Research* 20(4), 473–501.

—(1996) Computer-mediated communication: impersonal, interpersonal and hyperpersonal interaction. *Communication Research* 23(1), 3–43.

Walther, J. B. & Boyd, S. (2002) Attraction to computer-mediated social support. In C. Lin & D. Atkin (eds.) *Communication Technology and Society: Audience Adoption and Uses*. Cresskill, NJ: Hampton Press, pp. 153–88.

Walther, J. B. & Burgoon, J. K. (1992) Relational communication in computer-mediated interaction. *Human Communication Research* 18(1), 50–88.

Walther, J. B., Anderson, J. F. & Park, D. (1994) Interpersonal effects in computer-mediated interaction: a meta-analysis of social and anti-social communication. *Communication Research* 21(4), 460–87.

Walther, J. B., Van Der Heide, B., Kim, S. Y. & Westerman, D. (2008) The role of friends' appearance and behavior on evaluations of individuals on Facebook: are we known by the company we keep? *Human Communication Research* 34, 28–49.

Warschauer, M. (2004) *Technology and Social Inclusion: Rethinking the Digital Divide*. Cambridge, MA: MIT Press.

Watzlawick, P., Beavin, J. B. & Jackson, D. J. (1967) *Pragmatics of Human Communication: A Study of Interactional Patterns, Pathologies and Paradoxes*. New York: W. W. Norton.

Wellman, B. (1988). Networks as personal communities. In: Wellman, B. & Berkowitz, S. D. (eds.) *Social Structures: A Network Analysis*. Cambridge: Cambridge University Press, pp. 130–84.

(1999) From little boxes to loosely-bounded networks: the privatization and domestication of community? In J. Abu-Lughod (ed.) *Sociology for the Twenty-first Century*. Chicago: University of Chicago Press, pp. 94–114.

Wellman, B. & Gulia, M. (1999) Virtual communities as communities: net surfers don't ride alone. In M. Smith & P. Kollock (eds.) *Communities in Cyberspace*. New York: Routledge, pp. 167–94.

Wellman, B., Quan-Haase, A. Q., Boase, J., Chen, W., Hampton, K. & de Diaz, I. I. (2003) The social affordances of the Internet for networked individualism. *Journal of Computer-Mediated Communication* 8(3). (Online) Available at http://jcmc.indiana.edu/vol8/issue3/wellman. html (accessed October 1, 2009).

Welser, H. T., Gleave, E., Fischer, D. & Smith, M. (2007) Visualizing the signatures of social roles in online discussion groups. *The Journal of Social Structure*, 8(2). (Online) Available at www.cmu.edu/joss/content/articles/volume8/Welser/ (accessed October 1, 2009).

Whitty, M. & Gavin, J. (2001) Age/sex/location: uncovering the social cues in the development of online relationships. *Cyberpsychology and Behavior* 4(5), 623–30.

Who's Online (2009) Pew Internet and American Life Project, April. (Online) Available at http://pewinternet.org/Static-Pages/Trend-Data/Whos-Online.aspx (Accessed September 17, 2009).

Wiemann, J. M. & Knapp, M. L (1975) Turn-taking in conversations. *Journal of Communication* 25, 75–92.

Wynn, E. & Katz, J. E. (1998) Hyperbole over cyberspace: self-presentation and social boundaries in Internet home pages and discourse. *The Information Society* 13(4), 297–328.

Index of names

General index